EcoLaw

This book re-imagines law as ecolaw.

The key insight of ecological thinking, that everything is connected to everything else – at least on the earth, and possibly in the cosmos – has become a truism of contemporary theory. Taking this insight as a starting point for understanding law involves suspending theoretical certainties and boundaries. It involves suspending theory itself as a conceptual project and practicing it as an embodied and material project. Although an ecological imagining of law can be metaphorical, and can be highly imaginative and suggestive, this book shows that it is also literal. Law is part of the material 'everything' that is connected to everything else. This means that once the previous certainties of legal thinking have been dismantled, it is after all possible to think of law as 'natural' – as embedded in and emergent from a normative biophysical nature. The book proposes that there exists a natural *nomos*: animals, plants, and Earth systems that produce their own values and norms from which human norms and laws emerge. This book, then, proposes a new way to understand law, and pursues specific arguments to demonstrate the feasibility of law as ecolaw.

Drawing inspiration from current trends in the post-humanities, socio-ecological thought, and developments across the natural sciences in their specific intersections with humanities and social science disciplines, this book will appeal both to legal theorists and to others with interests in these areas.

Margaret Davies is Matthew Flinders Distinguished Professor at the College of Business, Government and Law, Flinders University, Adelaide.

EcoLaw
Legality, Life, and the Normativity of Nature

Margaret Davies

Routledge
Taylor & Francis Group
a GlassHouse Book

First published 2022
by Routledge
4 Park Square, Milton Park, Abingdon, Oxon OX14 4RN

and by Routledge
605 Third Avenue, New York, NY 10158

a GlassHouse book

Routledge is an imprint of the Taylor & Francis Group, an informa business

British Library Cataloguing-in-Publication Data
A catalogue record for this book is available from the British Library

Library of Congress Cataloging-in-Publication Data
A catalog record for this book has been requested

ISBN: 978-0-367-65199-2 (hbk)
ISBN: 978-0-367-65201-2 (pbk)
ISBN: 978-1-003-12833-5 (ebk)

DOI: 10.4324/9781003128335

Typeset in Times New Roman
by Apex CoVantage, LLC

To my mother Helen
and my sisters Catherine and Anne

Contents

Acknowledgements

I have been heading in the direction of this book for a few years but, were it not for the thoughts provoked by circumstances and events starting in 2018, would probably have continued to drift along without starting it. These circumstances included:

- a question from William MacNeil about whether my previous book was 'another version, albeit techno-pagan, of mediaeval natural law';[1]
- a comment reported by Jonathan Crowe that natural law needs to see 'nature as in some way normative';[2]
- reading Samantha Frost's inspirational book *Biocultural Creatures*;[3]
- an invitation to present a seminar at the Lismore Campus of Southern Cross University (Bundjalung Country) and the thought-provoking conversation that accompanied my presentation;
- the *Brave New Law!* Workshop (2018) and the Legal Geography Workshop (2020), both held at the University of Sydney (Eora Country)

My first debt of gratitude is therefore owed to all those who played a part in these provocations – who drew unexpected insights from my previous work, wrote significant books, and invited me to events.

A number of individuals – too many to remember and name – were present on the occasions mentioned above and contributed to the discussions that inspired me and helped me think through some significant issues. I would particularly like to thank William MacNeil, Jonathan Crowe, John Page, Alessandro Pelizzon, Greta Bird, Jennifer Nielsen, Aidan Ricketts,

---

1 MacNeil 2018, 138.
2 Hittinger, quoted in Crowe 2019, 15.
3 Frost 2016.

Susan Bird, Nicole Graham, Lee Godden, Tayana O'Donnell, Cristy Clark, Marc de Leeuw, Sonja van Wichelen, and Robyn Bartel. Throughout 2020 and 2021, the conversations continued, though generally online, and a number of people provided helpful suggestions, readings, seminar opportunities, feedback, and most importantly encouragement – these interlocutors included Rhys Aston, Davina Cooper, Anna Grear, Miguel Vatter, Vanessa Lemm, Daniel Matthews, Scott Veitch, Marco Wang, Desmond Manderson, Kathleen Birrell, Jana Norman, Samantha Frost, and, of course and as always, my dear and reliably curious friends Judith Gardam, Ngaire Naffine, Susan Magarey, and Sue Sheridan. In addition, I would like to thank the attendees and discussants at the Law and Inhumanities discussion group hosted by Hong Kong University in 2020, those who responded in one way or another to the Market/Place session within the 'For One Day Only' conference hosted by Lucerne University 2021, and the attendees at a series of workshops run by Hans Lindahl (Tilburg University) in October and November 2021. My collaborators in a different project ('Property as Habitat') – Lee Godden, Nicole Graham, and Laura Schuijers – have frequently raised and discussed ideas that have directly and indirectly been very helpful to developing the argument reflected in this book. I would also like to thank Colin Perrin for supporting the project and Kate Leeson for her thoughtful feedback and careful editing.

Although the institutional contexts that support scholarship can be difficult, I am thankful for the privilege that an academic life brings. Most notably, my conversion to a research-only position at Flinders University three years ago has brought with it the time to explore new ideas much more thoroughly than has been possible for me in the past.

I am immensely grateful to my partner Roz for her constant encouragement, her ideas, and for her inspiring vision of a home that welcomes, in segregated spaces, selected mammals as well as an extensive biomass, many plants, worms, butterflies, insects, reptiles, and birds. Most of the writing has taken place in the presence of our little dog Benny, whom I would like to thank for his generous affection and companionship and for frequently taking me away from my desk.

This book is dedicated to my mother Helen and to my sisters Catherine and Anne.

The book was written on the traditional lands of the Kaurna people. I acknowledge the profound inspiration of First Nations knowledges in my efforts to develop an understanding of law that aims for connectedness and resilience.

Introduction

Beginnings

A series of thoughts frame this book. First, 'we inhabit a *nomos* – a normative universe'.[1] As will become clearer, my image of the *nomos* refers to the idea that 'nature' – animals, plants, the Earth, and so forth – produces its own values and norms, and that human norms are part of this natural *nomos*. Second, the *nomos*, or normative universe, emerges from material processes but cannot be reduced to them in any mechanical sense. That is, norms emerge from the movement and interactions of matter at cosmic and geological scales, within life, and across ecosystems.[2] Third, emergent normativity is contingent yet stable and therefore accumulative (or, in social terms, historical) and constantly diversifying. This leads, fourth, to normalities and systems that are plural, complex, and intersecting, in short, that are ontologically entangled.[3] Relationship across normative scales (life, meaning, bodies, state law, microbes, Earth) is ubiquitous – the normative universe is interconnected and layered, not separated into bits. Legal systems and other human legalities are embedded within this universe, not

---

1 Cover 1983, 4; see also Delaney 2010 (on the *nomosphere*). Although 'nomos' is singular, for reasons of simplicity I sometimes use the term (ungrammatically) to denote a plurality of normative worlds. Moreover, I primarily use the term *nomos* in the sense in which it appears in contemporary legal theory, that is, to mean *law* and/or *convention*, sidestepping what Zartaloudis (2019, 20) – in his extraordinarily detailed and fascinating study of archaic forms of two antecedent terms (*nómos* and *nomós*) – calls its 'polyvalent forms and uses, which, in fact, do not lend themselves to universal definitions'.

2 Cf Bickhard 2004, who locates the 'base' of normativity in life. It seems clear, however, that developments in self-organizing complex systems, including nonliving systems, put the 'base' of normativity well beyond life. See Chapter 4.

3 Bartel 2017; Davies 2017b. Studies about the law-nature entanglement or co-becoming in particular fields are numerous. They include Pottage 1998; Gibson 2020; Arup 2021; Braverman and Johnson 2020.

DOI: 10.4324/9781003128335-1

separate from it. And finally, whilst normativity is in one sense co-existent with order, in fact order and disorder are not distinct, but are always co-implicated. Normativity implies sameness but relies upon difference, just as order implies system but relies upon disorder or chaos.[4]

I use the term 'ecolaw' to denote this interconnected and plural *nomos*. Ecolaw is not human law that governs the environment or ecosystems. It is not law for the Anthropocene or any system of legal governance at all.[5] It is an attempt to radically expand the referent of 'law' so that it is no longer an exclusively human system or plurality of human systems but unfolds with the matter of the universe (more particularly, of Earth). Thus, rather than expand legal subjectivity to animals and other natural objects, I aim to position law and normativity in general as ontologically prior to the designation of subjects and objects: everything becomes subject *and* object within plural normative relationships. Human beings are both subject and object in different normative worlds.[6] For instance, we are objects of a viral subjectivity even as we objectify viruses.

The distinction between, on the one hand, human law that regulates objects and, on the other, law that is emergent from interrelating things is critical. Much has been made in recent theory of Foucault's notions of biopower and biopolitics as the governance of life and of bodies by human regulatory systems. As Elizabeth Grosz explains, for Foucault 'biopower regulates a body from the outside'.[7] She points out that an alternative idea of biopower could refer to 'the powers that operate in and through living bodies'.[8] Although he did not deploy such a notion of *bio*power, Grosz reads Foucault as suggesting that *geo*power is power that is embedded in the Earth: 'Rather than concede geopower as the power that humans can extract from or hold over the geological, he sees geopower as the forces of the earth'.[9] With 'ecolaw' (and the sub-categories of 'geolaw' and 'biolaw') I aim to make an aligned distinction – the term does not refer to the limited domain of human law that *governs* life and the Earth, but rather to the unlimited domain of law that *emerges* from life and the Earth. Ecolaw connects biolaw, geolaw, and indeed human law. It requires a connection of legal theory with the science

---

4 Prigogine and Stengers 1984; Prigogine 1997.

5 Anthropocene-engaged legal theory edges much closer to my meaning, but still often has the tendency to relapse into thinking of law as *responsive* to Earth systems or as still regulatory over the Earth or planet as object.

6 In some ways a legal prioritizing of obligations over rights implies the priority of object status over subjectivity. See eg Davies 2016; Birrell and Matthews 2020.

7 Grosz et al. 2017, 134.

8 Ibid.

9 Ibid.

theory of recent decades. Science theory is in the process of supplementing mechanical laws involving deterministic cause-effect sequences with more probabilistic laws that engage agency, purpose, and constrained choice.[10] These developments make the connection of human law with the laws of nature much more credible, even unavoidable. In keeping with my previous work, I do not make a firm distinction between 'law' and 'norm'[11] – what is known in western legal theory as formal state-based law is emergent from, reliant upon, and ultimately blended into an extended *nomos* in all of its plurality and materiality.

In situating law in nature, there are undoubtedly some superficial parallels between what I present in this book from a western perspective and the knowledges of Indigenous peoples in Australia and elsewhere. I have drawn considerable inspiration and some terminology from the clarity and depth of Indigenous writing, artworks, and storytelling in communicating the connectedness of people to land and the emergence of law from land and relationships.[12] One motivation in writing this book is to help reorient western and in particular Anglo legal theory so that it is both more receptive to Indigenous knowledges and capable of acknowledging that many western 'discoveries' have been understood all along by Indigenous peoples, albeit in different forms.[13] With a few exceptions, however, I do not specifically draw on Indigenous sources. My purpose is not to construct a hybrid or synthesized version of the law-nature connection or even to specifically engage with the many forms of Indigenous knowledge, but rather to bring together resources within western philosophy and science theory for a narrative of ecolegality that is – like all eco-things – adaptive and adaptable. Any parallels therefore must be treated very carefully – my own theoretical outlook is situated within western theory and fails to touch on many significant dimensions of the rounded knowledges held by Indigenous peoples – the sacred, the located, the holistically embedded, the responsibilities of living. In addition to these limitations, my own theoretical horizon emerges from a genealogy still imbued with colonial and imperial attitudes, at the same time as I endeavour to resist these attitudes.

---

10 See eg Prigogine and Stengers 1984; Prigogine 1997.
11 Davies 2017b.
12 The central inspiration is the understanding of connectedness of law with land. One term I use throughout the book is 'co-becoming', which I first encountered in Bawaka Country et al 2016; other particular influences include Kwaymullina and Kwaymullina 2010 and the many works of Irene Watson (2000, 2017, among many others).
13 See eg Robinson and Raven 2020.

It is not possible to theorize human law as part of the extended *nomos* of physical nature without knowing anything certain about the latter. This poses a problem, as I have no background in science or science theory. Fortunately, there exists whole worlds of philosophy and theory undertaken by scientists, most of which is little studied in legal theory.[14] Perhaps even more evocatively, science practitioners are now more than ever writing about the philosophical meanings of their discoveries and hypotheses.[15] The book is an endeavour, in a partial and preliminary way, to bring styles of thought into legal theory that have originated in science but are not necessarily bound to it as a paradigm.

Argument

The story about law, nature, and normativity that I present in this book therefore begins with the order, disorder, adaptive properties, and emergent nature of earthly existence, both living and nonliving. The laws of nature and human law have in western theory often been regarded as radically different: on the one hand causally deterministic and necessary and on the other created intentionally and entirely contingent. But these particular meanings of 'law' are extremes. Human and nonhuman nature is more characteristically constituted by patterns that are 'normative' in the sense that they are comprised of continually emerging norms. Rather than focus on organisms, assemblages, or ecosystems, my emphasis is on understanding the norm-creating iterations and bonds that both create and disrupt the patterns of life and nonlife. To recap, to think of nature as normative means that it consists of a multiplicity of norms that have emerge from its many intersecting and unfolding processes.[16] A norm is a pattern, standard, or direction, that is also a guide for action. My working idea, to be elaborated more fully in the following chapters, is that norms – both legal and nonlegal, human and nonhuman – are iterative, connective, and teleological. That is, norms are the product of iteration or continued usage – things being done, thought, or spoken the same way repeatedly, though always accompanied by the potential for difference.[17] Norms are pathways created by usage or

---

14 With notable exceptions, of course, such as Donna Haraway, Bruno Latour, and Karen Barad.
15 See for example Gagliano 2018b.
16 For the living, such processes include evolution, adaptation, acculturation, symbiosis, learning, communicating, storytelling, and many others. For the nonliving, norm-creating processes are associated with the movements of matter and energy – various forms of flow, for instance.
17 See eg Uexküll 1934/2010, 98ff ('The Familiar Path').

movement:[18] they guide action but do not mechanically determine it. But norms also arise from exchanges, relationships, and bonds between organisms and between bits of matter.[19] Bonds constitute and differentiate. They are ligatures, obligations.[20] To use the legal terminology, norms, both human and nonhuman, are therefore basically habitual (customary) and contractual.[21] Finally, norms are aligned with and motivated by purposes, even if – in many instances – the purpose is forgotten, minimal, or buried. Teleology – purpose-driven action or action that follows a direction – as I will outline, is normative. It motivates norm creation. Norms, as opposed to the laws of physics, are always contingent in the sense that they could have developed otherwise. Moreover, they do not lead to determined results – there can always be, and often are, deviations, sometimes leading to new norms.[22]

The critical task for an ecological understanding of law is to replace law's objectifying and distinguishing strategies with an understanding of law that places it within the relationships that create it (along with everything else physical and conceptual). In order to elaborate this position, I take the extremes of physical nature and human law in the western tradition and, as it were, fill the gap that philosophy and legal theory has created and enforced between them by comparing their form and elaborating the position that what is understood as human positive law is entirely continuous with or situated within the physical world. What westerners understand as 'law' is in part a reduction and cross-section of material processes, though this materiality must also be understood as constituted through historical and cultural dynamics.

Law in/as Nature

'Material' is a complex word – it resonates with *matter*, which is also constrained energy,[23] as well as with meaning, which is of the mind, but is no

18 Davies 2017b, 144–153.
19 Serres 1992, 38; Latour 2017, 64; Margulis 1967, 2010.
20 As Karen Barad 2010, 265 says: 'Entanglements are not a name for the interconnectedness of all being as one, but rather specific material relations of the ongoing differentiating of the world. Entanglements are relations of obligation – being bound to the other – enfolded traces of othering'. See also Yusoff 2013; Veitch 2021.
21 Intentionally created norms and laws are an exceptional and derivative, rather than a central or original, case of norm: norms that are intentionally created always rest on existent norms already established by conventions and relationships.
22 See in particular the discussion of Canguilhem in Chapter 3.
23 See the explanation of this point in Frost 2016, 31–41. Frost 2016, 35 says:

> What we know or experience as matter is energy whose differentiation produces highly constrained forms of self-relation. Those highly constrained forms of energetic

less material for being so.[24] Materiality is not static but moves according to a tempo specific to its spacetime and metabolism. What thinkers in the western tradition have understood as 'nature' is equally, if not more, problematic and encompasses (among other things) various models of human nature, pastoral versions of the natural world found in nineteenth-century romanticism, misogynist and racist ideas that associate women and non-white people with a passive physical world and a non-rational animality, as well as the objectified 'factual' physical nature of natural science.[25] Both 'law' and 'nature' are cultural constructs that are intended to refer to something 'real' but the characteristics of the reality and the narratives that constitute these constructs, not to mention the endlessly mobile human position as situated agent in this web of natural-legal materialities make this a difficult set of relationships to untangle.

My argument situates what is understood in mainstream legal theory as the separate sphere of law in its ecological context. I intend to describe and illustrate the myriad ways in which the reified 'law' of the state and its institutions is produced by its material, including its biological, surroundings and to give texture and dimensionality to its pluriversal qualities. A similar argument has been made – repeatedly – about the ways in which law is a product of social (that is, human) relationships and performances.[26] However, once matter is fully engaged in a theoretical analysis it is very difficult – impossible actually – to sever the nonhuman from the human. Over the past decades, legal geographers have been at the forefront of moving beyond the human and exploring the emergence of law from place, an emergence that is necessarily dynamic and hence temporal.[27] Such work theorizes humans and our legal performances as embedded first and foremost within

---

self-relation are the conditions for the generation of various forms of extension, density, endurance, and dimension, some of which are beyond human perception but some of which we humans experience as heavy, light, staid, evanescent, solid, fluid, airy, opaque, or transparent.

See also Barad 2012.

24 On the 'entanglement of matter and meaning' see generally Barad 2007. See also Ahmed 2008, discussing Butler 1993, 33.

25 Classic critiques of the nature – culture division with all of its scientific mythologies and gendered/racist connotations include Merchant 1980; Lloyd 1984; Plumwood 1993.

26 I have elaborated this position at length in Davies 2017b, but it had already been asserted by generations of legal realists, legal consciousness scholars, and certain legal pluralists. See eg Llewellyn 1931; Ewick and Silbey 1998; Sarat 1990.

27 Blomley 2003, 2013; Delaney 2010; Bartel 2017; Graham 2011; Braverman et al 2014; Philippopoulos-Mihalopoulos 2015; Bartel and Graham 2016; T O'Donnell et al 2020; Braverman and Johnson 2020.

places, together with the multidimensional materialities of specific localities. This book takes a slightly different slice of materiality (the biological, the ecological, and the geological) but retains the focus on understanding the nature of law and normativity that I have previously pursued.

Situating human law within the broader socio-ecological (including geological and potentially cosmic) does not mean that there is any straightforward relationship between the norms of nature and the norms and laws of human societies. Scientific narratives, like philosophy and social theory, have often reflected the grand assumptions and preferences of modernism, now in the process of being displaced by more complex narratives:[28] prominent examples include the Cartesian story that nonhuman nature is mechanical;[29] the individualizing tendencies of liberal thought reflected in organism-centric investigations of life;[30] or the sovereign governance model once attributed to the genome.[31] Darwin's comments about the 'struggle for existence' are a fascinating case in point. Is this a struggle against other individuals for scarce resources or is it a collective struggle in difficult conditions? Or is it something of both? In 'Kropotkin was no Crackpot' Stephen Jay Gould documents a divergence between early twentieth-century Anglo-American and Russian evolutionary theory which, to a degree, followed geo-political tendencies.[32] Evolutionary theorists in the Anglosphere emphasized the struggle as a competitive battle primarily conducted by individuals (and, later in the century, by their selfish genes). By contrast, the early Russian followers of Darwin took a different approach, acknowledging individual struggle, but also looking for collectivism, co-operation, and, in Kropotkin's terms, 'mutual aid'.[33] Kropotkin's anarchism was directly informed by his appreciation of the advantages of collectivism in evolutionary struggle.[34] It appears that, for Kropotkin, animal nature was not only a model for the possibilities of human politics, but also continuous with it.

At the same time, human law clearly cannot be deduced isomorphically from a 'book' of natural meanings like a medieval bestiary. Just as narratives embedded in human cultures (for instance to do with competition or

---

28 Turner 2013, 189 says 'it would be fair to say that scientific, social, and political spheres were all shaped together by a peculiar mutualism'. See also Stengers 2010, 2011.
29 Henning and Scarfe 2013.
30 Gilbert et al 2012.
31 See eg Lappé and Landecker 2015; de Leeuw and van Wichelin 2020; Dupré 2013, 32.
32 Gould 1988, with reference to Todes 1987.
33 Kropotkin 1902. Lynn Margulis 2010 based her work on symbiosis on the earlier work of Russian microbiologists, which had been largely ignored in the Anglosphere.
34 Dugatkin 2011.

co-operation) cannot be used simply as an interpretive lens for nature, nor can natural norms be translated directly into the human socio-legal sphere. This is not to say that the norms of the natural world are never instructive. Sometimes, for instance, they can be used to cast doubt on human prejudices, such as the alleged alliance between heteronormativity and nature. Nonhuman sex and sexuality prove to be far more complex than human heteronormativity.[35] The territorial behaviours of certain animals are highly suggestive for thinking about human constructions of territory and property.[36] Georges Canguilhem, whose work I use frequently in this book, distinguished human law from the vital norms of organisms more sharply, arguing that the latter are 'immanent, present without being represented, acting with neither deliberation nor calculation'.[37] The normative pluralities that form an organism (or superorganism, or holobiont) are not consciously chosen or followed. They emerge without reflection. Human law, by contrast, can be identified, represented, intentionally followed (or not), and reformed. This workable conceptual distinction between the immanent norm and the representable is not, however, so easily maintained in a material sense, given that all human law is established upon the grounds of both culturally embedded (and therefore neither immanent nor external) human norms as well as nonhuman norms that are the product of billions of years of accumulated planetary change.[38] It is true that human state-based law is produced though processes external to a single human body and that it can even be written down and digitized, but what of this? The human, after all, is already an assemblage of symbiotic and autopoietic processes and is, moreover, not only a being but a becoming,[39] an ongoing process of constitution from quite different materials. Law needs to be interpreted by different 'minds' which in themselves are materially shaped by the physical world,[40] and hence this separate human law potentially takes multiple forms. It achieves any stability it has only through the actions of human bodies acting in groups – through their conversations, arguments, decisions, written communications, and so forth. Externalized state-based law never

---

35 See eg Hird 2006 (on 'animal transex'); Hird 2009, 91–115 ('microontologies of sex'); cf Barad 2010 on the queer properties of electrons.

36 See eg Deleuze and Guattari 1987, 311–318; Gibson 2020, 105–131; Bradshaw 2020.

37 Canguilhem 1966/1978, 154. See also Genel 2021.

38 See eg Norman 2021, 116–118.

39 Lambros Malafouris 2010, 49, for instance, uses the term 'human becoming' in his analysis of 'metaplasticity' – 'the enactive, constitutive intertwining of neural and cultural plasticity'. See also Malabou 2008; Pottage 2015. I discuss autopoiesis and symbiosis/sympoiesis as they have been used in relation to law in Chapter 5.

40 Malafouris 2010, 2013.

escapes the immanent norms from which it has developed, whether these are at the quantum level, the cellular and microbial, the behavioural, or the cultural. The interactions and intra-actions that produce norms are rarely linear.[41] The multiple intersecting normative systems of a complex normative ecology produce disruptions, detours, and hybrid norms at every step of the way.[42] Thus it is never possible to reduce human culture, politics, and legal deliberation to nature, but nor is it possible to separate human beings and our natures from nonhuman nature. Plural normative systems form both continuities and discontinuities between normative matter and human meanings.

Strategies and Methods

As I have already mentioned, ecosocial norms are produced by habits and bonds, by pathways and symbiosis, and have a purpose or direction in the sense that they give order to movement. There is a plurality of norms, a plurality of potential normative worlds, and a plurality of normative fields across biological, geological, and social (human and nonhuman) planes. The point of departure of this book is ecosocial:[43] it brings together the ecological and the human/social by viewing these multiple planes of normativity as connected and mutually constitutive, even though – for analytical purposes – they are frequently studied and analysed as separate. Since my disciplinary reference point is law and the social norms that inform law, I have extended a conceptual language of normativity that (in my view but not everyone's) resonates with the legal sphere, even though it is not exclusively drawn from that sphere. This conceptual language does not apply in a straightforward way to other disciplines, especially not the biological and physical sciences. How then is it possible to bring law, human social norms, and the norms of the natural world into a common framework? Two related strategies inform my approach. First, I *compare* socio-legal normativity with nonhuman normativity: that is, I interpret nonhuman order using some of the conceptual tools of socio-legal thinking. The second angle involves developing an appreciation of the *continuity* of human and nonhuman normativity and a perspective that situates all human norms within a wider

---

41 'Intra-action' is Karen Barad's term for the actions or movements from which dynamic phenomena materialize. Rather than thinking of entities relating or interacting, intra-action names the continual connections that produce things as ongoing processes. Barad 2007, 137–141.

42 Cf De Landa 2000; Murray 2008; Ruhl 1996; Finchett-Maddock 2017; Murray et al 2019.

43 Or 'socio-ecological'. See generally Code 2006; Philippopoulos-Mihalopoulos 2013.

nonhuman context. My focus is continuity since, in this field, *dis*continuity is a given – but, in fact, here as elsewhere, continuity and discontinuity co-exist.[44]

In this way, my analysis relies on reading the concept of normativity across nonhuman settings in a way that scientists might find jarring or inaccurate – for obvious reasons, I do not claim to add substantive knowledge to the nonhuman world as such, only to frame scientific knowledge in a particular way and to use natural science as a 'thinking ground' for an approach to normativity in the living and the nonliving. Canguilhem said, 'life is in fact a normative activity'.[45] And moreover, '[w]e do not ascribe a human content to vital [that is, living] norms but we do ask ourself how normativity essential to human consciousness would be explained if it did not in some way exist in embryo in life'.[46] In other words, the interacting complexity of human normativity depends on a more basic biological normativity that exists well beyond the space occupied by the human being. Viruses, for instance, also have their norms, as they are driven to replicate and do so according to established patterns. These viral norms are clearly not separate from human life and human norms but rather interact with them, for better and for worse. Looking even further, past biology to nonliving processes, Ilya Prigogine said, 'human creativity and innovation can be understood as the amplification of laws of nature already present in physics or chemistry'.[47] As I will outline in Chapter 4, Prigogine's research in physical systems has allowed incredible depth and detail to be observed and understood in the continuities and connections between nonlife and life, and between nonhuman and human.

How is it possible to understand this continuity of the normativity of the nonliving, the living, and the human within the terms offered by legal theory? The dominant assumption, practice, and idiom about law, derived from legal positivist theory, is that law is largely conceptual. Despite the inbuilt requirement that law *become* practical at some point, in this perspective law is nonetheless often regarded as having a life of its own as abstract: law's substance, though expressed via the physical medium of language and memorialized in permanent form as documents,[48] is regarded as mental and

---

44   See eg Barad 2010 on quantum and queer 'dis/continuity'.
45   Ibid.
46   Ibid. See also Barham 2012.
47   Prigogine 1997, 71. The most detailed exposition of human-nonhuman dynamics using complexity theory that I am aware of is De Landa 2000.
48   The physical elements of language are often erased in theory, but it is helpful to remember that one of the critical early interventions of the 'linguistic' turn in theory concerned the

conceptual. Law may have its origins in social relationships but is conceptually detached from them. Strongly associated with the view that law can be distinguished from material practices, and in some way precedes them or governs them, is that it is singular and state-based – there is one law, one state and sovereign, one territory, one legal world. By contrast to top-down and conceptual approaches to state-based law, the pragmatic, sociological, and anthropological traditions in legal thought, as well as much of the critical tradition, are more likely to explain law as having a material basis: as emerging from the relationships of humans in their specific communities and located in place and time.[49] Even where formal law is recognized within such approaches as the construct of a politically superior institution and therefore somewhat autonomous from society at large, it is nonetheless situated in and interpreted by reference to social meanings and everyday practices that are necessarily place-emergent and historically located. As socio-legal thought extends legality beyond positive law, so eco-legal thought extends legality beyond the human.

My strategy for thinking through the continuity of normativity across these differentiated spheres is very straightforward. It simply involves a shift in orientation from a human-centric focus to a matter-centric focus. Looking past the taxonomies that enforce the human-nonhuman divide necessitates that we see that these spheres – while separable for some purposes – are nonetheless unified by matter and the processes that shape it. There is no getting away from human dependence on the physical world, living and nonliving, and, since this is the case, an explanation of law that is confined to the human is only telling part of the story of law. The *physicality* of human bodies conversing and acting with others – in physical locations, with and in relation to physical objects – is not always foremost or even present in positivist and even in critical socio-legal accounts of law, but is nonetheless necessary to them.[50] As I have mentioned, legal geography stands out among the critical traditions for integrating law with place, where both law and place are understood as comprised of matter and practices that are social, historical, and ecological. It therefore engages directly with the nonhuman and physical elements of the emergence of law. Theoretical approaches to law based on material practices tend to avoid depictions of

---

materiality of language. See eg Coward and Ellis 1977; Derrida 1981b; Barthes 1972; Althusser 1994; discussed in Davies 2017b, 51–54.

49 Ehrlich 1962; Pound 1910; Falk Moore 1973; Ewick and Silbey 1998; Cover 1983; Grbich 1992.

50 See eg Kelsen 1967, 2 ('law – or what is customarily so called – seems at least partly to be rooted in [physical] nature and to have a "natural" existence').

law as logical, systematic, or singular: as emergent, law is necessarily based on diversity and contestation as well as on the singularizing and reifying impulses of its more abstract discourses.

In one sense, the point that human normativity is situated within natural normativity is obvious, even trite. If the human species is simply part of an extended biophysical sphere (an obvious point) then everything that is *of* the human sphere is also of the natural sphere. We humans are a subset of a larger set, represented diagrammatically as a circle within a circle rather than as a circle that intersects with another circle. But discussions about what is 'right' in a social or legal sense are often dissociated from the biological substratum of normativity, from the fact that life itself is a normative activity and that, as I will argue, norms and normalities are produced in nonliving matter as well. The dominant legal narrative about norms has been that they are independently authorized rules that a rational person can understand and decide whether to follow. However, social rightness must be emergent – at least in part – from already given bio-socio-cultural norms. To say that something is 'emergent' means that it is constantly in production from the complex interactions of a substrate – it comes from a set of material relationships and cannot be separated from them. This does not imply that the emergent thing is only the sum of its parts, rather the opposite.[51] So-called moral norms, for instance, can be seen as the product of several intersecting and cumulative factors. These include: evolutionary adaptations that are themselves based on the iterative trial and error of reproduction and finding what works for a particular environment;[52] socio-cultural adaptations that are similarly responsive to place and environment; historical and economic transitions; intellectual rationalizations of social, political, and other (eg religious, economic, etc) characteristics; and politics and concentrations of power. To dissociate morality from human history, from long-term adaptations to time and place, and from movements between organism and habitat, community and environment, seems to remove the preconditions for any notion of rightness.

Because the human being is an organism, and in fact a 'living system',[53] the material explanation of law cannot stop at merely *human* relationships.

---

51 For an extended discussion see Stengers 2011, 207–233.
52 De Waal 2014; Joyce 2014 discusses the distinction between those who argue that moral judgements are the product of biological adaptations and those who argue that they are the product of psychological elements (which are themselves 'quite possibly adaptations') such as the ability to make abstractions, to see consequences, to understand the suffering of others, and general social instincts.
53 Maturana and Varela 1980.

There is no boundary that can be drawn around the human organism in a material sense.[54] There are, of course, many discursive and mythological boundaries that have been placed around human organisms and human societies, especially in western thought. However, as we are seeing all around us, the image of isolation from our habitat and broader environment is a destructive myth. 'We have never been individuals' (as one biology article aptly puts it).[55] Law as an ecological phenomenon emerges from trillions of micro-actions of such living systems in specific places and times.[56] This constant activity, like the biochemical reactions that generate it, forms patterns and stabilities that over time materialize as 'law'. There is nothing that is 'law' that does not emerge from this material context or that can be explained or understood without it. Even the most idealist and conceptual understanding of law cannot divorce it from the physical 'natural' world.[57] Everything that we refer to as 'law' emerges in a context of physical action even though it is reified into an abstract form.

Chapter Outline

The chapters that follow expand upon these points. Because this is a short book, they are introduced and opened up for exploration, rather than thoroughly argued and defended. **Chapter 1** is essentially introductory. It begins by taking an apparently extra-legal biological phenomenon – slime mould – and considers a series of questions. How it is possible to conceptualize the relationship between slime mould and human laws? How is slime mould materially connected to human law? What are the normative qualities of slime mould? Can the idea of normative pluralism extend beyond plural

---

54 Frost 2016.
55 Gilbert et al 2012; cf Norman 2021.
56 Davies 2017b.
57 For instance, the legal idealist Kelsen 1967, had trouble removing law from its physical substance:

> society, understood as the actual living together of human beings, may be thought of as part of life in general and hence of nature. Besides, law – or what is customarily so called – seems at least partly to be rooted in nature and to have a 'natural' existence. For if you analyze any body of facts interpreted as 'legal' or somehow tied up with law . . . two elements are distinguishable: one, an act or series of acts – a happening occurring at a certain time and in a certain place, perceived by our senses; an external manifestation of human conduct; two, the legal meaning of this act, that is, the meaning conferred upon the act by the law.

See Davies 2017b, 44–46.

human systems to nonhuman worlds? The second section of the chapter provides some further groundwork for the argument relating to the facticity and normativity of nature, and a more thorough explanation than that provided in this introduction of the (tentative) model of normativity used in this book. The third section of Chapter 1 consists of a brief overview of the bio-, geo-, and human registers of normativity.

Chapter 2 turns to ideas of nature and teleology. 'Nature' is a highly contested term in theory and, in adopting the term, one can never hope to navigate fairly the many – and sometimes conflicting – meanings with which it has been invested. Nonetheless, and possibly imprudently, after consideration of some of these problems I forge on with using the term, largely because there is no viable alternative. Much of Chapter 2 sketches philosophical approaches to the question of whether (and how) the physical natural world can be said to be purposive or directed and hence teleological. As I have mentioned, purpose or direction is the critical motivator and defining feature of normativity whether manifested as making, following, accepting, resisting, or re-forming norms. Some appreciation of the history of the philosophy of teleology in nature is unavoidable. The chapter tracks in outline a trajectory starting with Aristotle to the rise of mechanistic anti-teleological thinking in the early modern era, to Kant's discussions of the apparently teleological nature of organisms, and finishing with Schelling's rejection of the objectification of nature.

Chapters 3, 4, and 5 follow a familiar (though intrinsically contestable) division of the material into the biological, the geo-logical/graphical, and the human.[58] Chapter 3 considers two early twentieth-century bio-theorists who imagine different aspects of what it is to be a nonhuman being. Georges Canguilhem theorized the life of organisms as a process in which immanent bio-norms are constantly made and re-formed. He rejected the idea that there was an essential normality or static set of norms that could be used to characterize an organism. Rather, the norms of the organism's 'normal' are made by the organism itself as it works to avoid suffering and enhance wellbeing. Hence 'diversity is not disease' but rather, possibly though not always, a stage in the creation of a new normal. Jakob von Uexküll offered an even more remarkable dimension to this imagining of what it is to be a nonhuman organism. He invited his readers into animal and insect worlds, imagining their *Umwelt* or subjective bubble of meaning, as it is formed through receiving perceptual signals from and engaging with external things. The resulting image of plural phenomenal worlds adds a

---

58 See eg the structure of De Landa 2000.

second-order layer to the immanent bio-norms described by Canguilhem. It is from the experience of interiority that arises in *Umwelt* that the plural semiotic worlds of living collectives arise; hence the emergence over eons of patterns that give rise eventually to cultures, exteriorized structures, institutions, and bureaucracies.

Normativity does not stop with life, and Chapter 4 expands the analysis to nonlife. The chapter starts by considering some philosophical and scientific methods of distinguishing between life and nonlife: matters discussed include plasticity of form, different ways of occupying spacetime, the ability to self-organize, and causal determinacy. However, the material continuity of life and nonlife carries equal significance to the distinction between them. The other substantive section of the chapter looks at the image and actuality of material *flow* as a significant feature in the construction of norms. Although many things flow, I focus on water and energy. Water is perhaps the nonliving resource that to date has intersected most explicitly with western law via the recognition of nonhuman rights. But underpinning everything is energy dissipation, which can be attributed with a nascent and ongoing normativity across all Earth-bound processes.

I turn to human law in Chapter 5. More specifically, I look at some selected questions in legal theory that connect to the themes of the book – first, the materiality and relationality of what we understand as (hypothetically separate) positive law; second, the idea of nature in natural law theory; and finally, the idea of legal co-becoming as it has been considered in socio-legal and more recent socio-ecological thought. This final section of the chapter also looks at autopoiesis as a biological metaphor for legal system closure and sympoiesis as an alternative biologically grounded language for the co-construction of human-nonhuman normativity.[59]

---

59 With particular reference to Grear 2020; Petersmann 2021.

1   A New Living Law

Introduction

Consider the slime moulds.[1] They are both microscopic and macroscopic organisms, neither plant, animal, nor fungi, that are known to have around a thousand different species. Slime moulds are notable for their variable aesthetics, their amazing shape-shifting abilities, their ecological functions, their mobility, their biophysical properties, and their many social capabilities. To look at, slime moulds come in several forms.[2] Some visible slime moulds are relatively flat plasmas without individual cells but multiple nuclei that stretch like irregular webs or crackle patterns across surfaces such as logs. Others with a similar acellular structure form irregular lumps, such as the aptly named 'dog vomit' or 'scrambled egg' slime. Others are microscopic single cells but under certain environmental conditions (lack of food, mainly) they form visible superorganisms.[3] The most beautiful of these make a little trunk consisting of thousands of sacrificed individual organisms at the end of which sits a polyp of dormant spores waiting to burst out when conditions are more favourable. Slime moulds can be a single colour, or multicoloured, and many are iridescent.

Slime moulds have generated a significant quantity of academic literature in many science disciplines, not only the disciplines of biology but also cognitive science, information science, bionic engineering, evolutionary theory, materials science, immunology, ecology, cybernetics, and others. But they have also become interesting for systems and network theory,

---

1 See generally Lloyd 2018.
2 A large number of images can be found in Lloyd 2018 and also online.
3 A 'superorganism' is a collective of interdependent organisms that form a whole, such as an ant colony, a beehive, the human body, or – in some accounts – Gaia. (On why Gaia cannot be described as an organism, see Latour and Lenton 2019.)

DOI: 10.4324/9781003128335-2

as well as a medium for artists, musicians, and a general inspiration for curious thinkers. This interest is a consequence of the remarkable properties of slime moulds. They exhibit collective and social behaviour, even though they are acellular or single-celled organisms. They can radically change shape to look like webs or slugs and can move across different terrains. They can learn, sense, remember, and make decisions,[4] for instance to find the fastest route through a maze, even though they do not have neurons. Their cognition and behaviour are organized distributively rather than concentrated in a central cell or group of cells. One mould species has the properties of a 'memristor' or a material that remembers the pathway of an electrical current.[5] Slime moulds can process information and form optimal networks between a complex set of points. These and other properties give them many applications in computing and artificial intelligence.[6] In early 2020, an algorithm based on a slime mould growth pattern was used to map with a high degree of accuracy the connections between galaxies.[7]

Despite their many practical applications and remarkable capabilities, as organisms slime moulds seem a long way from humans and an even further distance from human law. But they are in many ways instructive;[8] they challenge the human- and higher-animal-centred images that pervade cultural ideas about cognition, individual identity, and social behaviour; they provide information about the evolutionary connections between amoeba and humans; they have worked themselves into human culture and theory; speaking broadly, their patterns and modes of being may have much in common with human life.

So what can we say about the connection of slime mould with law? How do law and slime mould interact? Legal theory suggests several possibilities, drawn from the expanding jurisprudence on animals, insects, microorganisms, and plants.[9] Looking at the question from a conventional legal point of view, even in the absence of a category of 'slime mould law', there is obviously much in law that might reference the slime mould: what law allows humans to do and not do, for instance in changing land uses that

---

4 Reid et al 2012; Beekman and Latty 2015. The use of terms like 'learning' may be controversial for forms of so-called primitive cognition that are not neuron-based. See generally Moskovitch 2018. However, in appreciation of its problem-solving abilities, one US college has appointed a slime mould faculty member: Resnick 2018.

5 Braund et al 2016.

6 See generally Adamatsky 2016.

7 Burchett et al 2020.

8 Fox Keller 2007b.

9 Many imaginative and critical approaches regarding animals are presented in Otomo and Mussawir 2013, eg Philippopoulos-Mihalopoulos 2013. On plants, see eg Roncancio 2017.

affect slime mould ecosystems; or the various regulatory mechanisms that banish unwanted organisms from human-occupied spaces such as hospitals, hotels, houses, and schools. Can slime mould be used for human purposes and appropriated in the form of some product or patentable invention?[10] From this straightforwardly legal perspective, the slime mould would be a target of legal regulation – probably excluded from law's direct notice rather than specifically named, but nonetheless a passive recipient of legal action, appropriation, exclusion, protection, or nonaction. Like much of the nonhuman sphere, it is an *object* affected by the norms of human subjects. Extending this slightly, slime mould (and other parts of Earth's ecosystems) inhabits human meaning and therefore can be regarded as potentially part of the wider human *nomos*, or normative world.[11]

The change of orientation required by ecological thinking inspires a second set of law-slime mould connections, that is, concerning the material entanglements of humans and all of their institutions with the nonhuman world. Meanings emerge from the material world and humans also emerge as beings from this world. Everything human belongs to material ecologies; as first and foremost physical beings we are entirely reliant on our habitat and environment, all of it, including the slime. Thinking ecologically requires a repositioning, a flattening, of the subject and object: no longer in charge, no longer unique, no longer essentially individual, the human circulates in distributed ecological networks in which we are always becoming rather than being. We are ontologically object as much as subject, although we assume the position of subject and reify it through social forms and legal institutions.[12] In itself, slime mould, or any other organism (or collective-individual superorganism), might be understood as an assemblage of intra-actions that are also networked into other socioecological assemblages, in which human meanings and materialities also participate.[13] Ecologically motivated legal theory has so far had little impact on the modalities through which state law operates in practice,[14] though some legal effects are to be seen wherever the human is placed by law in a relational context or where the environment is promoted as an end in itself.

---

10 Cf Limon 2013.
11 Cover 1983.
12 See eg Marwani 2019 (on insects as 'biopolitical agents').
13 Cf Philippopoulos-Mihalopoulos 2015; Arup 2021.
14 But see important theoretical contributions aimed at improving state law responsiveness to the natural world by situating law and regulation within a socio-ecological context: Kotzé 2019, 2020; Kotzé and Kim 2019; Petersmann 2021; Brooks and Philippopoulos-Mihalopoulos 2017; Parker and Haines 2018.

Increasingly, efforts are being made to see natural entities not only as vulnerable objects requiring protection, but as subjects and partners in new legal relations.[15] Michel Serres, for instance, speaks of a natural contract in which the whole of humanity relates symbiotically as contracting partner with the Earth: 'we must add to the social contract a natural contract of symbiosis and reciprocity'.[16] This is possible because 'the Earth speaks to us in terms of forces, bonds, and interactions, and that's enough to make a contract'.[17] Latour clarifies that Serres' natural contract 'is not a deal between two parties, humanity and nature'. Instead, it is 'a series of transactions in which one can see how, all along and in the sciences themselves, the various types of entities mobilized by geohistory have exchanged the various traits that define their agency'.[18] The natural contractual bond is immanent to every planetary thing because it precedes the emergence – via symbiosis and/or intra-action – of entities and agents. As Whitehead succinctly put it: 'We are in the world and the world is in us'.[19] There can be no objectification of the Earth as other in such a contract, much less its erasure in property or a property-like construct, because we are all symbiotically bonded. As contract, it is not individualistic but fully relational: transactions can only be understood in the context of the relations that make them possible.[20]

A third angle that arises as soon as we start to think of ourselves (potentially and provisionally) as objects to nonhuman subjects concerns the experience of living organisms and the agency of the nonliving. This is not a topic that is widely explored in legal philosophy. However, the hard boundary between human and nonhuman has been constituted within a subsection of human epistemology (roughly, the European subsection with its specific cultural, social, and political dispositions). Whatever the merits of separating human from nonhuman for some purposes, to view the distinction as ontological or foundational in any way is problematic. Human life must

---

15 Clark et al 2019, 830–844; Anker 2017; Davies 2015, 224–229. Many arguments for animals to be recognized as legal subjects and rights bearers have now been overtaken by the attribution of legal personality and rights to parts of nature or to nature understood as interconnected complex systems. A summary is available in Clark et al 2019.

16 Serres 1992, 38. See also Grear 2020; Akhtar-Khavari 2020. Serres implies a difference between the current situation of parasitism, in which humans abuse and drain the Earth's resources, and symbiosis, which he sees as more equal. My limited reading suggests that parasitism is usually regarded as one form of symbiosis: see Gilbert et al 2012, 328.

17 Serres 1992, 39.

18 Latour 2017, 64.

19 Whitehead 1938, 165.

20 Macneil 1999.

also be seen as only one part of an ecological society and (to avoid species solipsism) the experiential world of nonhuman life must therefore be
drawn into the understanding of human worlds, including our law. Like the
human world, the wider worlds of nonhuman life are composed of norms,
perceptions, creativity, and cognition. Biologist Lynn Margulis writes:
'consciousness, awareness of the surrounding environment, starts with the
beginning of life itself'.[21] Such awareness, however minimal, was attributed
world-creating capabilities by bio-theorist Jakob von Uexküll.[22] According
to Uexküll, every organism produces an *Umwelt* (that is, its own subjective
phenomenal environment[23]) which is the product of its perceptual world
and the effects it creates in that world. The organism has its own subjective
'bubble' of experience, meaning, and material engagement constituted by
the process of receiving perceptual signals from the physical surroundings
and creating effects which become the organism's environment. Some such
bubbles are simple and formed from just a few connections, such as the
microbe whose sole perceptual signal is received from things it bumps into
and swims away from until it comes to rest on something it can eat.[24] The
COVID-19-causing coronavirus has a key that enables it to unlock a cell in
order to enter and replicate, thereby participating in endless still-unfolding
ways in human societies, politics, economies, and imaginaries. The human
or the dog, by contrast, have multiple perceptual signals and multiple effects
they can create in the material world.[25] Whatever the level of complexity,
all are constituted by the organism in the 'functional cycle' between itself
as subject and the objects in its world.[26] In this way, the organism creates
its own world and its own time and space – time and space are created by

21 Margulis 2001, 58.
22 An Estonian biophilosopher whose major works were written in the 1920s and 1930s.
    Despite his exquisite descriptions of the subjectivity of animals such as ticks, molluscs,
    microbes, dogs, and many others, Uexküll incongruously promoted the idea of a natural
    grand design that was anti-Darwinian and creationist. See Uexküll 1934/2010.
23 The term *Umwelt* is often translated as 'environment' but the obvious problem with this
    is that 'environment' in English can be over-extended to connote an objective external
    expanse rather than the subjectively constructed world of the organism itself. Many prefer
    to retain the term *Umwelt* so that its more precise meaning – which connotes a perceptual
    and semiotic bubble for the organism – can be better assured. Indeed Sutrop 2001, 448
    remarks that this extension of the term has in fact occurred in German and that the 'philo-
    sophical meaning of the word Umwelt is preserved now only in English'.
24 Uexküll 1934/2010, 73.
25 Along similar lines, Whitehead 1938, 166 wrote: 'I find myself as essentially a unity of
    emotions, enjoyments, hopes, fears, regrets, valuations of alternatives, decisions – all of
    them subjective reactions to the environment as active in my nature'.
26 Uexküll 1934/2010, 50.

the organism in its management of the different events that take place in its *Umwelt*. These worlds are not entirely self-referential or separated from others' worlds but intersect, overlap, and disrupt the worlds of others.[27] The notion of *Umwelt* represents a dramatic and extremely clear coming together of what classical philosophy has distinguished as ontology and epistemology: the organism's corporeal existence, its perception, and therefore its world, its norms, and cognition are inseparably constituted.

I will come back to the plurality of subjective worlds, nonhuman and human, in later chapters. At this point, however, we can flag a fourth dimension of the law-slime mould relation by thinking about the existence of multiple *normative* worlds.[28] Normative pluralism is well understood in socio-legal theory and in legal philosophy. That human societies live according to plural legal and normative systems, often co-located territorially and forming hybrid normative orders within groups and individuals, has been much studied. In recent scholarship the concept of legal pluralism has been developed so that it refers not only to relatively autonomous co-existing systems of norms, but to more complex interactions between layered, intersecting, mobile, and heterogeneous normative practices.[29] The concept of legal pluralism has not ordinarily been extended to the intersecting plural normative worlds of nonhuman life,[30] but it is an apt translation of pluralism to do so. The normative plurality of the intersecting worlds of nonhuman organisms is perhaps best left to ecologists, without the added filter of legal pluralism. But insofar as humans and human law are entangled in the multiple pluralities of socio-ecological being, then the idea of normative pluralism is helpful. The organism is part of the extended material environment in which normativity arises but also has its own subjective experience and meanings derived from its engagement with that world. How does the organism live its life normatively and what is its *nomos*? What is its purpose, for itself, for its group, and for the ecosystem? Of course, we will

---

27 Deleuze and Guattari 1994, 185 say that Uexküll developed a 'melodic, polyphonic, and contrapuntal conception of Nature'.

28 The literature on the pluriverse is expanding, but an early and generally overlooked precursor is María Lugones, whose 'Playfulness, "World"-Travelling, and Loving Perception' (1987) provided a different analysis of multiple oppressions to the better-known intersectional theory. More recently, see Law 2015; Law and Lien 2018. The application to law is explored by Aston 2020.

29 Griffiths 1998; Melissaris 2009; von Benda-Beckmann and Turner 2018; Davies 2017a.

30 But see Bartel 2017 (pluralism of place-generated law). Insofar as pluralism involves a plurality of human normative worlds that include Indigenous cosmologies, the nonhuman is of course 'included' in pluralist thought. However, the orientation and entry point for pluralism has been the human connection.

never actually know its own meanings or subjective experience but, considered with an imaginative gaze informed by but not slavishly bound to the objectifications of science,[31] the organism has a teleological and therefore normative existence. It lives according to norms, and can even create new norms for its life in order to survive, adapt, and flourish.[32] As Georges Canguilhem explained, such 'vital normativity'[33] defines change in organisms: 'In biology the normal is not so much the old as the new form, if it finds conditions of existence in which it will appear normative, that is, displacing all withered, obsolete, and perhaps soon to be extinct forms'.[34] Slime mould, like all organisms, is characterized in part by an inherent normativity that might help illuminate human normativity – as Canguilhem argued, organisms create and follow norms. It might even be said that biogenesis is jurisgenesis. Both processes, after all, rely on abundant production and selective survival of normative pathways.[35]

Insofar as human law is understood as a separate regulatory sphere (a common but hardly universal understanding of law) it therefore constructs the living world; it shapes, categorizes, and determines it. But that is only the beginning of the story that connects law and 'nature'.[36] Combining material ecological connections, the subjectivity and the normativity of each living thing, the normativity of ecosystems at large, and the *nomoi* of nonlife and the Earth at large, it is possible to hypothesize a dynamic image in which all law, including the formal law of nation-states, is completely enmeshed in socio-ecological practices. Human law is constituted as such by multiple intersecting and co-constitutive socio-ecological normative fields, from microbes to artistic endeavours, to philosophy and forests.[37] Intellectually, this image of intersecting plural normative worlds is only an extension of the well-established, but human-centred, studies by legal anthropologists and sociologists of the ways that human *nomoi* – living law, cultural narratives, everyday normative practices, and socio-legal plurality – are

---

31 Science feminism from the 1980s, notably the continuing work of Donna Haraway, has been influential here. See eg Haraway 1988, 2016; Frost 2016; Code 2006, especially the description of 'ecological naturalism' at 90–94.

32 Canguilhem 1966/1978; Okrent 2017.

33 Explained in detail in Chapter 3.

34 Canguilhem 1966/1978, 82.

35 Cover 1983; Margulis and Sagan 1995, 24.

36 The term 'nature' is clearly problematic in many ways but I have chosen to retain it, usually with qualification or clarification as to its meaning in a specific context. Even so, 'the first reflex of every critical tradition consists in fighting naturalization': Latour 2017, 21.

37 On forests, see Clark and Page 2019. On geo-pluralism see Bartel 2018 discussed below, Chapter 5.

connected to and inform formal law. Any difference from a socio-ecological legal pluralism and that which has previously been studied flows from the human-nonhuman boundary. To many, this boundary might appear to be an insurmountable obstacle, especially when thinking of something as formalized as singular state-based legal systems. Maintaining the boundary begins (but does not end) with the human itself: it involves glossing over the human body and the myriad of relationships and trillions of micro-organisms that constitute it and maintain it. Slime mould is part of an ecological world and arguably part of the *nomos* within which humans exist as organisms defined by their sociality and their individual and collective legality.

It is therefore possible to include in ecosocial legal thinking the subjective experiences of organisms ordinarily regarded as outside the human domain, as well as the norms they create and follow to maintain their life and reproduce, and their meaning making in the physical world and in relation to other subjects that situate the organism in an ecosystem. This extension of the *nomos* provides a wider frame of reference for the assemblages of law produced by normative becoming.[38] The idea of the 'chronotope' as deployed by Mariana Valverde (drawing on Bakhtin), is helpful in this context. A 'chronotope' is an ordering of space and time through the relationship of heterogeneous things (such as texts, inter-textual relations, and practices, both emergent and embedded). Reified socio-legal things, such as 'the honour of the Crown',[39] can be understood as chronotopes that engage in and contribute to further socio-legal ordering. The term (and Valverde's analysis) can equally be useful in thinking of living-nonliving orderings: any organism is, after all, a complex ordering of heterogeneous matter-energy-meaning into a specific spatiotemporal form. As Carl Woese famously said: 'Organisms are resilient patterns in a turbulent flow – patterns in an energy flow'.[40] An organism is resilient, but also contingent and open, and reliant on other orderings – other spatiotemporalities – both 'within' and 'outside' its apparent boundaries. From the chemical flows that constitute metabolism, to the microbes that assist or undermine biological functions, to social connections, location in geographical place, its long evolutionary development, and many other entanglements, an organism is chronotopically complex, intensely temporal and spatial, but has no ontological fixity. By contrast, classical natural law eschews space and time: it is grounded nowhere and said to exist everywhere and at all times, in the same

38 Valverde 2015.
39 Ibid, ch 5.
40 Woese 2004, 176.

form.[41] Classical natural law is therefore the antithesis of the chronotope. Rather than a 'thickening' of space and time,[42] it thins out spacetime so that it barely exists.

These several modes of thinking about the law-slime mould relationship are neither mutually exclusive nor comprehensive. There is no system to be found that could adequately capture in its totality the social-ecological meanings and properties of the emergent living world. This is not only because 'meanings' and 'properties' cannot be disentangled but also because of their differences in space and time: across human culture and in different and changeable physical locations. Norms are not 'in' space and time but emerge with the processes that make spacetime meaningful and orderly. We use norms – of perception, imagination, communication – to describe and account for other norms and normativity in general. This does not imply circularity, but rather density and entanglement, at the same time as openness and escape. Normative fields are heterogeneous: multidimensional, conflicting, and intersecting, but nonetheless emergent from material practices. Most importantly perhaps, is that in nature both meanings and properties continually develop and reshape themselves. Whilst some organisms might be ancient, they nonetheless continue to evolve. In any event we – the living things on planet Earth – are always in a state of becoming in our social-ecological systems. But can normative plurality be imagined at this scale?

'Normative' Nature

To say that nature is normative and plural is to contradict the classical and now frequently contested assertion that nature is singular and factual. Embedded in the claim that nature is normative is a further assertion: that nature is vital and agential, active and emergent, rather than passive or mechanical. Flow precedes substance.[43] These ideas are not necessarily very difficult to comprehend. After all, even a single plankton, or a single virus, follows and recreates the norms of its existence. It acts and engages normatively; that is, doing or not doing what it ought to do, not making conscious choices but perhaps – for some organisms – choosing nonetheless or at least responding and engaging with habitat and *Umwelt*.[44] There are

---

41 Finnis 1980; but cf Crowe 2019; Davies 2019.
42 See Valverde 2015, 10.
43 Nicholson 2018; see also Schelling 1799/2004, 18; Lucretius 2001; below Chapter 4.
44 See generally Canguilhem 1966/1978 (discussed in Chapter 3); cf Barham 2012; Okrent 2017.

multitudes of relationships and hence plural worlds for the many beings in existence,[45] not to mention the plural cultural ontologies lived by human communities. It is therefore, in one sense, easy to comprehend the normativity and plurality of biological nature. What is more difficult to untangle are what might be termed translational matters: how can the normativity, agency, and plural worlds of living things be understood in relation to the conceptual landscapes of western philosophy? In what ways are nonhuman normativities part of a human *nomos*? Can the normative responses and relationships of a plankton be compared to those of a human and a legal system? In what ways is its agency comparable to human agency? How does plurality sit with science? The extended *nomos* does not end with life, only to be taken over by purely causal physical laws. Rather, normative Earth systems – and the big composite of multiple systems, Gaia[46] – are composed of agential, patterned, and purposeful nonliving as well as living matter.

Facts and Norms

One of the most significant obstacles in western thought to a theory based on process and becoming is the fact-value or fact-norm distinction. As is well known, the Scottish philosopher David Hume warned against deriving an 'ought' from an 'is'.[47] Hume's so-called guillotine became a fixture of subsequent philosophy, and was undoubtedly exaggerated by many. Franz De Waal points out that Hume's language is qualified, suggesting care and a search for reasons before judgements about oughts are made on the basis of facts.[48] It does not imply a bright-line distinction. However, the traditions of philosophy, science, and jurisprudence in the Anglosphere have often been guided by a fixed imperative of avoiding any confusion between facts and norms, and in particular the alleged confusion between is and ought.[49] This became a critical issue in the dispute between natural law and positivism. In law, positivist theorists, who (dubiously) claimed to be able to describe law as if it were just a set of facts,[50] claimed that natural law theory improperly derived moral norms from something merely factual – human nature.

---

45 Uexküll 1926, 1934/2010; see also Law and Lien 2018.
46 See eg Latour 2017.
47 Hume 1740/1969, 521.
48 De Waal 2014.
49 See eg Austin 1954, 184.
50 Ibid; Kelsen 1967, 1991.

Natural law theorists countered that there was no such illicit inference in their work.[51]

The fact-norm (or fact-value) distinction has been a cornerstone of modernist thought beyond legal theory,[52] but whether or not it is defensible depends on framing and context. (As Ruth Anna Putnam observes, even '[t]he notion of a fact . . . is hopelessly fuzzy'.[53]) Clearly, for instance, experience and science (social and natural) have determined 'facts' about the world that are true beyond any reasonable doubt (to use the legal standard) even if they are sometimes also referred to as theories and put into doubt. If I jump off a chair I will descend, I can't cut a diamond with a plastic knife, life evolves, multiple massacres of Aboriginal peoples were committed in Australia until at least the 1920s,[54] the benefits of vaccines far outweigh any harms, and the global climate is warming as a result of human activity. These facts or explanations of facts are backed by substantial evidence and widely accepted as facts. Sometimes, accepting facts and sound explanations is a critical step and it is equally imperative to resist disingenuously manufactured or distorted facts.[55] This does not, however, imply that facts are necessarily singular, that there is even a unified world of facts, or that description of facts can be value-free and neutral – clearly my selection of facts implies a politics, for instance. The intellectual disintegration of the fact-norm distinction does not mean that it can or should be abandoned in every circumstance.[56] It does mean that there is a need to be careful and as clear as possible about the parameters of facticity and objectivity. More than ever, we need reliable, if provisional, means for establishing agreed truths.

Within the paradigm of objective facts, in which human knowledge describes and represents data packaged as facts, these can be established with a high degree of certainty. But the stance of an objectivity that is universal, unlocated, and disembodied is, to quote Donna Haraway, 'fantastic, distorted, and irrational'.[57] Writing in 1988, Haraway argued for a kind of knowledge that would recognize the relationships between subject and object, consisting of a starting point in which the observer is situated (obvious when you think about it) and the object has agency.[58] Universal

---

51 Finnis 1980, 33–48.
52 See eg Marchetti and Marchetti 2017.
53 Putnam 2017, 105.
54 Ryan et al 2019.
55 Latour 2004.
56 Haraway 1988; Latour 2004, 2014.
57 Haraway 1988, 587.
58 Ibid, 591–592.

knowledge and unsituated objectivity is a limited paradigm that does not account for the agency of ourselves in the construction of facts or in 'the very existence of the phenomena those facts are trying to document'.[59] Moreover, the paradigm of unsituated objectivity fails to account for non-human agency – that is, far from representing something other, being and knowing (anywhere, anything) consists of a co-becoming, an emergence of people and things as such.[60] Things that have sometimes been perceived as passive data ready for observation and description are agents and even subjects insofar as they engage, resist, and change in response to things that humans do. In such a context, there is no unvarnished fact but rather a dynamic and purposive emergence. As I will explain, normativity is embedded in processes of emergence – in all forms of material becoming.

Recognition of the agency of nonhuman things is now a commonplace in ecologically oriented theory. Another emerging theme that is less common but nonetheless increasingly found in the literature is the attitude of plurality not only in our human cultural perspectives (what was once known as cultural relativism) but also in our ways of engaging and knowing, and in the worlds we produce – that is, in our ontologies as well as our interpretations.[61] It is for this reason, along with the more conventional reasons, that 'nature' has become such a highly contested term. As mentioned above, until recently, the idea of 'nature' underlying natural law theory, and also found in much moral and political philosophy, consisted largely of *human* nature (and a somewhat distinctive version of human nature). The 'nature' that belonged to science at least *seemed* to be observable, and scientific theories were consequently falsifiable. The 'nature' of natural law theory has no such empirical basis, making it reasonable to ask whether there has ever been any 'nature' in natural law thought.[62] I will return to natural law theory in Chapter 5.

---

59 Latour 2014, 2.
60 Ibid, 5; Haraway 1988, 592 says:

> Situated knowledges require that the object of knowledge be pictured as an actor and agent, not as a screen or a ground or a resource, never finally as a slave to the master that closes off the dialectic in his unique agency and his authorship of 'objective' knowledge.

For an elaboration of co-becoming, see Bawaka Country et al 2016.

61 The becoming into being of different worlds is evident in phenomenology, and has been taken up in feminist theory, for instance, by María Lugones 1987. Lugones spoke of the 'world' travelling undertaken by minorities and the political and emotional attitudes that accompany different ways of being and perceiving in different worlds. For a philosophical analysis see Carlisle 2017.
62 See eg Kerruish 1983. Crowe 2019 represents a move towards updating natural law theory in this regard.

By contrast to both the conventional scientific and the natural law versions of nature, within an ecocritical or ecophilosophical attitude, 'nature' cannot be so singular – it cannot be a 'One World World'.[63] We are, for instance, faced with the undeniable truth that many Indigenous ways of knowing and being are more ecologically coherent, more aligned with, and less destructive of ecosystems than the approaches of the 'civilized' west. There is no 'nature', only 'natures', and since this plurality of natures is a co-*becoming*, it is not merely a question of perspective or epistemology but rather of ontology (or, as Karen Barad says, 'onto-epistemology', in recognition that being, knowing, and becoming are products of indistinguishable processes).[64]

Defining Normativity and Norms

I will expand upon the normativity of these plural natures in later chapters, but a few more words about terminology are needed.[65] There is an unfortunate though probably unavoidable lack of clarity in usages of the term 'normative'. This is because this adjective broadly means 'pertaining to norms' or 'about norms' but in a legal theory context it is used to refer to an evaluative argument about what the law *should* become. A 'normative' argument aims to improve the law, by reference to some social, economic, ecological, or other standard. 'Normative', or reform-oriented, arguments are contrasted with 'descriptive' or doctrinal analysis of what the law is. However, as many critical legal theorists have argued, so-called descriptive accounts of law are already or can easily become norm-laden. For instance, not only is law situated within a context in which colonialism has been normalized, not only does this law often reflect the norms of racism and patriarchy, but it is interpreted and applied with tools and presumptions that invisibilize these framing norms.

In addition to the contrasting meanings of 'pertaining to norms' or 'goal oriented' are other meanings of 'normative', to do with the process of judgement and the creation of norms. Georges Canguilhem put it like this:

> *Normative*, in philosophy, means every judgment which evaluates or qualifies a fact in relation to a norm, but this mode of judgment is essentially subordinate to that which establishes norms. Normative, in the fullest sense of the word, is that which establishes norms.[66]

---

63 Law 2015; see generally De la Cadena and Blaser 2018.
64 See Law 2015; Barad 2007.
65 See also Davies 2017b, 36–38.
66 Canguilhem 1966/1978, 70.

In this book, I use Canguilhem's 'fullest sense' of 'normative' to refer to *processes which create norms* in an evolving *nomos*. Norms are patterns, standards, and directions, that are also guides for action. *Facts* and norms can be constituted as separate for strategic reasons (for instance to improve the law) but they remain part of a single plane of becoming, process, or emergence. Dissolution of the fact-norm distinction in a philosophy of emergence or constant change implies that there is (for instance) performance or action that is at once normative and factual and that is responsive to an existing normative landscape, at the same time as it is purposive and creative of the present and future.

There are several different ways of dissecting the term 'norm' and its adjective 'normal'. As a noun, 'norm' means at least two things. First, 'norm' describes a material convergence, normality, or regularity, for instance of social behaviour or linguistic usage. As Canguilhem said, 'The norm of norms remains convergence'.[67] Second, a 'norm' is a rule or guide for behaviour, external to individual norm-following agents – such a norm can be imposed at a point in time, as in legislation or an order from a superior, but the vast majority of existent norms are not imposed, but emerge through time from social, biological, and possibly even geological processes. (And even those that are imposed rely on a pre-existing complex of emergent bio-socio-geo-norms.) Similarly, 'normal' can mean the average or standard and it can be a judgement about a thing: the two senses appear to be different but clearly they are related since a judgement that something is not normal, like the judgement that something is 'not natural', is often part of the socio-political process of enforcing normality. Norms therefore encourage converging behaviour, the process of normalization. Part of this process is the suppression or marginalization of difference/deviance. Such a view of norms has its most obvious exponents in twentieth-century French philosophy, as Katia Genel explains. She says, 'Canguilhem and Foucault mostly view socially accepted norms as standardizing processes of normalization that stifle normativities that do not conform'.[68] Canguilhem located such normativity within the organism, whereas Foucault (influenced by Canguilhem) located it in socio-political-historical dynamics. We can see a similar structure of the norm in Derrida's elaboration of iteration as the marker of signification.[69]

---

67 Ibid, 153.
68 Genel 2021, 72.
69 See generally Chapter 3.

Norms can therefore be found in material regularities, in connections, and in explicit standards and rules. Regularities are embedded in matter and in practices, while explicit standards are abstracted from regularities and/or independently laid down as rules. It is in the transition from the first to the second sense that facts and norms become indistinct. Simply, if something happens regularly, and is 'normal', that is a fact. However, the mere fact that it is normal means that it very often is or becomes a guide for behaviour: 'Everyone understands the power of the status quo not only to perpetuate itself but also to legitimate itself'.[70] As regularities, norms have a stickiness or gravity that encourages further convergence. In the human sphere, imitation clearly plays a role in the creation of and reproduction of norms, as does reason (do what works for a particular goal), and reified concepts of normality and deviance.[71] It is not that stickiness is a property of norms, of course. It would be more accurate to say that norms are a property of, or the consequence of, a certain sort of stickiness – that which produces convergence.

The initial reasons for the convergence that creates a norm undoubtedly vary according to context; one material instantiation or event helps to produce a second and – from there – a pattern, habit, or self-repeating process. Drawing inspiration from process philosophers Henri Bergson and AN Whitehead, Ilya Prigogine demonstrated such norm-producing capacities in what physicists call 'far from equilibrium' open systems,[72] such as weather patterns. Some fluctuations in the movement of matter come to nothing, but others are magnified and reinforced, bifurcating, ordering themselves, and becoming more complex.[73] Self-organizing systems are norm-creating systems: they produce probability-based norms rather than the causal necessities of the mechanical laws of physics. In his vast exposition of physical and social order, *The Self-Organizing Universe*, Erich Jantsch expressed a general principle of norm emergence applying to both the human and the non-human: 'The transformation of novelty into confirmation may be observed at all levels of the micro- and macroevolution of life on Earth'.[74] Jantsch

---

70 Stolzenberg 2010, 116.
71 Canguilhem 1966/1978; Foucault 1967.
72 See Prigogine 1997, especially Chapter 2. In very broad terms, this refers to systems in which there are imbalances of some sort – for instance temperature or air pressure – resulting from new inputs (matter, energy, information) from the environment. Earth is a far from equilibrium open system because it is constantly receiving new energy from the sun. Organisms are also such systems.
73 Ibid.
74 Jantsch 1980, 228. See also Schneider and Sagan 2005, 103. Jantsch's work was based on the earlier work of Prigogine.

often uses 'normalization' as a synonym for 'confirmation'. Novel elements are introduced into a system, some of which are repeated and confirmed, leading to norms and normalized patterns. Because such order emerges out of existing patterns and systems, it is necessarily temporal and historical – a norm might appear to be a singular thing at a point of time, but it is in reality an emergent force, compressing all of the iterations that preceded it.[75]

The idea that norms arise from the repetitions of custom is embedded within the common law. Law was seen in the early centuries of the common law as emerging from usage since time immemorial or since 'time out of mind'.[76] The legitimacy of such law was sometimes said to be based on this unremembered origin, but it was also understood to be based on solid social regularities and tried and tested behaviours.[77] Similarly, beyond the formal law, social norms often, though perhaps not inevitably, emerge from regular behaviour and the imperative to behave normally. Repetition of a fact creates a norm or pattern which creates a norm or guide for behaviour. Like the common law, habitual behaviour may stabilize because it works towards a particular goal and/or because it is efficient, a shortcut or heuristic. For instance, pathways that are etched into the land because they are the most efficient way to reach a destination (whether by a person or an animal) can also be seen as norms – they literally show the way to go.[78]

Critical and social accounts of performativity complicate the picture of norms as habits that are socially mandated, by deploying an understanding of repetition as iteration.[79] The actions or performances that create and embed social norms (such as the myriad norms associated with gender) do not consist of repetition of the same, but also of difference (which may be more or less amplified, but is always there):[80] thus, repetition creates *and* subverts the 'normal'. A subtle difference in the performance of a social role may, over time, alter the norms associated with it. Nonetheless, in order to be legible as a performance, it must also reproduce these norms sufficiently. The idea of the norm therefore consists of repetition of the same and of the difference that is inherent in repetition. It is necessarily dynamic and ongoing, not static. The creation of norms through material repetitions and

---

75 The association of emergent order with irreversible time was regarded with hostility by those wedded to a Newtonian mechanical view of the universe, as Prigogine 1997, 61–62 describes.
76 Sir John Davies 1612 Irish Reports in Pocock 1957, 33; see generally Postema 1989.
77 See eg Hale 1778/1971; Duxbury 2017.
78 Davies 1992, 2017b, 144–153; Barr 2016.
79 Derrida 1981a.
80 See eg Butler 1990; Blomley 2013.

convergences in the presence of otherness, plurality, and potential alternatives, resonates strongly with the ways in which the norms of life and the orderliness of nature in general emerge, as I will explain in more detail in Chapters 3 and 4. Thus, a further complication of the simple view of normativity as usage is that habits and the norms embedded in them subsist in *all* of the (inseparable) dimensions of our being and knowing: not only do they exist in bodily processes, and our location and orientation in the physical world and in social customs,[81] but also in language, cultural formations, and perception.[82]

But norms are also produced in relation: what is variously termed bonding, correlation, co-becoming, co-operation, contract, inter- and intra-action, symbiosis, and sympoiesis.[83] These relational activities involve merging and diverging entities that are connected in some way, exchanging resources such as nutrients, electrons, or DNA, communicating, forming social structures, or reproducing. At the legal scale, a contract forms a set of norms for the relationship between the contracting parties and/or may make a new legal entity:[84] contractual norms can emerge over time in a pattern of mutual behaviour, or they can be intentionally agreed with a signing ritual, a handshake, or a simple quid pro quo. A contract produces mutual obligations between a self and an other, which may be relatively fair and equal, or can be asymmetrical as a result of built-in differences in bargaining power and other environmental factors. But an obligation can also be entirely one way, attached to a role or position, or emergent from actions such as negligence. In Roman law, an obligation was a *vinculum juris*, a legal 'fetter, bond, chain, or rope'[85] that tied the person with the obligation to the person they owed it to. Commenting on Latour's analysis of law, Kyle McGee says: '*Vincula juris* are those bonds, cords, laces, links on which the force of law travels: they make up the "wiring" system, cables strung up behind the walls of the totality'.[86] Relationality – as physical or metaphorical ties – is now understood to be not only constitutive of all law and the autonomous identities that inhabit it,[87] but of socio-political and cultural patterns and persona. At the scale of the norms of matter and of life, new norms created by relating are in constant production: if a seed lands in a

---

81 Ahmed 2006.
82 See eg Okrent 2017; Doyon and Breyer 2015; Delaney 2010, 15.
83 See eg Grear 2020.
84 Veitch 2021, 63.
85 Birks, quoted in Veitch 2021.
86 McGee 2015, 478.
87 Nedelsky 2012.

healthy microbial soil a pattern of material exchanges is quickly established between microbes, fungi, plant, and atmosphere. Symbiotic relations more generally enable and structure life at every stage from the formation of cells to entire ecosystems. Such symbiotic normativity is not necessarily separate from the normativity produced by repetition but is often co-extensive with it. Entities and normalities emerge in symbiosis which is itself reliant on regular patterns already established (just as the contract relies upon existing conventions, such as those to be found in communication, in the monetary system, etc). Repetition and connection are 'mechanisms' that give rise to norms, but they are also interleaved and inseparable.

A derivative type of norm that emerges out of this extended substratum of complex, networked, and ubiquitous normativity around us is commands or instructions given by one agent to another. Such norms include instructions from employers, enactments of a legislature, parental directives, or any number of socially generated prescriptions. Modern positivistic concepts of law downplay the idea that norms arise from any kind of usage or convergence of action but the primacy of social and ultimately nonhuman normativity in the analysis of legal norms is unavoidable. As guides for behaviour norms are typically seen by positivist theorists as emerging from some kind of authoritative action (eg a command or edict)[88] but, if these are to count as 'legal' norms, they must nonetheless rely on conventions and usages, on actions and social fabrics, that allow, inform, and support them.[89] It is well established that law does not (and cannot) operate or even exist simply as explicitly intended acts of autonomous human will. All law is dependent on social and linguistic norms, as well as on repeated material facts and embodied actions. There is no legal norm that can be expressed or understood without the prior substratum of embodied social norms within which it was produced. The construction of any law can only occur out of the actions of ecologically interconnected and embodied beings.

---

88 Kelsen 1991, 3 says,

> Even though the adjective 'normal' contains the root 'norm', it does not refer to an Ought but to an Is. Something is 'normal' if in fact it occurs regularly. When people use the term 'normal' to signify an Ought, they presuppose that there is a valid norm to the effect that what usually happens ought to happen, and in particular that people ought to behave as they are used to behaving. . . . It is a fallacy to infer from the fact that something in fact regularly happens, that it ought to happen. No Ought follows logically from an Is.

89 Davies 2017b.

Bio-norms, Geo-norms, and Human Norms

Norms then, are produced in endless, interrelating, iterative movements of things from the microscopic to the communal to the ecosystem, and even to the cosmos. 'Norming actions' give rise to and entrench norms by iteration and connection. Norms are iterative or performative, and hence emergent through fact and action and bringing time and space together in movement: imposed (sovereign-generated) norms are always secondary to emergent norms, because they rely upon an already existent and already quite complex norm-creating process.

I use this schematic idea of normative action, a co-becoming of fact and norm (iterated facts become norms, facts are nonetheless never free of prior norms), to connect qualitatively different planes of norming, from the geological to the legal. In terms of tradition, the reference point is Ehrlich, rather than Kelsen – norms are alive, in life, and ingrained in facts.[90] Bio-norms, for instance, emerge from the processes of life, including the pathways, relationships, patterns, and regularities that constitute organisms and ecologies. They are not separate from or prior to the social-symbolic registers of 'culture'.[91] Bio-norms are produced in the co-becoming of organism and habitat and in the self-regulating systems of 'autonomous' living agents. Living norms produce autonomy from multiplicity and multiplicity from autonomy and arise in the bonds formed by cross-species interaction and formation. Bio-norms also emerge from directed actions, to grow, to survive, or to avoid pain.[92] The purposive character of life has vexed many philosophers and scientists in the Cartesian tradition, who have preferred to see the entire nonhuman world as mechanical and who have rejected teleology as implying supernatural design, inherent forms, singular ends, or states of perfection.[93] But to speak of teleology in this context does not imply motivation either by a beginning (such as a creation or even an intention) or an end (such as a final or perfect condition). Nor does it imply singularity or linearity. Teleology is direction[94] – for self-preservation or for transformation. It is also more accurate to speak of teleologies in the plural

---

90 See Van Klink 2009.
91 Frost 2016; Landecker and Panofsky 2013.
92 Canguilhem 1966/1978; Frost 2016, 149.
93 For instance, Kant sets out an antinomy in the *Critique of Judgement* to capture the problem that nature requires mechanical explanation but that as 'natural ends' organisms appear to elude such explanation. I discuss mechanical, vital, and teleological accounts of nature in philosophy and science in Chapters 3 and 4, with particular reference to Aristotle and Kant. See generally essays collected in Henning and Scarfe 2013.
94 Samantha Frost 2016, 85 speaks of 'direction-without-intention' rather than teleology.

because they are complex – intersecting, disruptive, multiple. The danger with the term 'teleology' is that it comes with so much conceptual baggage, but I use it because the alternatives ('teleonomic', 'telic') are unfamiliar and less connected to philosophical traditions.

Directed action and emergent normativity are also apparent in nonliving things. For many, this point is more controversial than the norm-producing nature of life. Eurocentric thought has for centuries endeavoured to maintain a boundary around life, insisting on the passivity of nonliving matter.[95] Ontologies that do not accept this division are abundant, but such worlds have been mainly invisible to Eurocentric thought, especially to its science and philosophy. But, as Jane Bennett comments, 'it might be only a small step from the creative agency of a vital force to a materiality conceived as itself this creative agent'.[96] A number of disruptions to the life-nonlife boundary constitute a series of 'small steps' towards their reintegration:[97] the evident participation of heterogeneous material things within meaningful human networks;[98] the physical entanglement of things and humans;[99] the difficulty of defining life; and the agency of nonliving things in transformations of matter. It is not only life that has force.

But is the agency of nonliving things a *normative* agency – that is, does it create and follow norms? Despite challenges to the life-nonlife boundary, a line has nonetheless often been maintained between the laws of nature that (in the language of analytical philosophy) have nomic necessity and in which purpose or directed action plays no part and the teleological or purpose-driven norms of life. However, even this boundary is now contested. Pre-biotic chemistry is understood to have a purposive component; many natural processes are understood to be temporal, irreversible, and probabilistic (and therefore pluralistic and evolutionary);[100] and interconnected Earth systems (Gaia) follow non-deterministic, self-created, directed patterns.[101] Connecting physical and biological science, Margulis, Sagan, Schneider, and others have argued that there is continuity between life and nonlife on the basis of the 'telic' or purposive nature of energy dissipation and its interesting connection to the ongoing emergence of life.[102] 'Life . . .

---

95 See the account by Whitehead 1938, Lecture 7 'Nature Lifeless'.
96 Bennett 2010, 65.
97 Povinelli 2016, 14 says 'a posthuman critique is giving way to a post-life critique'.
98 For instance, as documented by studies informed by Actor-Network Theory.
99 Hodder 2012.
100 Prigogine and Stengers 1984.
101 Lovelock and Margulis 1974; Margulis and Lovelock 1974.
102 Schneider and Kay 1994; Schneider and Sagan 2005; Sagan and Margulis 2013. Bickhard 2004, 130 states: 'All of mind and mental and social phenomena are fundamentally

appears to be a particular instantiation of a general natural process, the formation and spread of materially-cycling systems in regions of energy flow'.[103] Life does not *contradict* the tendency of energy to spread and matter to decay even though – as Erwin Schrödinger famously explained – it creates order out of disorder.[104] Rather, according to the view informed by non-equilibrium thermodynamics, life *channels* energy flow. Moreover, human teleology (and hence normativity) can be situated within the framework of energy transitions: 'Our telic behaviours stem from those of nature'.[105] These matters will be further explored in Chapter 4.

Conclusion

Human norms are more obviously iterative, connective, and teleological than physical processes. Legal norms are often seen as explicitly imposed rather than produced through repeated practices or embedded in relations. However, even state-defined law, with its intentionally constructed parliaments and rules imposed from a position we imagine as 'above' everyday life and outside the self nonetheless rests on a bedrock of long material practice and convention. It emerges from human bodies and neural patterns embedded in complex social practices produced over millennia and in quite different temporal scales and environmental situations.[106] In *Law Unlimited*, emphasizing the extended materiality and plurality of human law and normative practices, I described law (provisionally) as:

> discursive, performed, assumed, located, relational, and material. [Law] is emergent in social space – through performances, intra-actions, and material relations, and also through the imaginings, narratives, and self-constructions that inform and are informed by these things. Law is inside and outside the self, material and immaterial, immanent to mind and body, and in natureculture. It is intrinsically plural – differentiated

---

normative, and they all emerge in a hierarchy with biological functional normativity at its base. Some other locations and levels in the hierarchy include representation, perception, memory, learning, emotions, sociality, language, values, rationality and ethics'. The thermodynamic explanation of life proposed by Schneider and Kay, Sagan, and Margulis puts the normative 'base' beyond biology, in energy dissipation.

103 Sagan and Margulis 2013, 213.
104 Schrödinger 1944/1992.
105 Sagan and Margulis 2013, 228.
106 I have written about these points in detail in Davies 2017b.

by different knowledges, subjectivities, locations, performances. It is also solid and fluid – predictable, merely probable, but also contestable and transient.[107]

This idea that laws – state laws and other modes of normativity – are emergent from plural material relationships and practices serves as a point of departure for this book. In this book, however, I have a greater focus on the nonhuman sphere and its continuities with the human. For practical purposes, institutional and imagined lines are drawn around human law, which enable it to function as a discipline and technique in the human sphere. Even as such a practice, the looseness of its edges is well known. But there is no need for theory of law to be bound by these demarcations (although theorists have so often imposed these strictures upon themselves), and hence the intrinsic open-ness of human law can be exposed to the full engagement of humanity with the world.

107 Ibid, 89.

2 Teleologies of the Nonhuman

Introduction

Everything is connected, everything is a product of relating, everything is normative, and everything changes. Norms are patterns, processes, and guides, which are the effects of ecological forms of relating. They emerge from the dynamics of becoming and associating. Human bodies, identities, lives, societies, and institutions emerge, at every scale of existence on Earth, from the matter of biological and physical processes. Far from being a reductive account, a materialist and posthuman account of law and nature brings into one space all aspects of existence, including the norms and signifiers of the cultural worlds we each inhabit. Living beings are in the physical world together, collectively, but we can be situated in different ecosystems and different ontological worlds. These overlap and often collide. The proposition that I support in this book, that 'nature is normative', crosses the diverse meanings of 'norm', 'normal', and 'normative' discussed in Chapter 1. To rephrase it in the simplest fashion: nature (by which I broadly mean the pluriversal nature of human-nonhuman worlds) produces and consists of norms. Norms are dynamic regularities – constantly re-forming patterns – that emerge from and promote sameness and convergence but also allow (indeed are based upon the possibility of) difference and divergence. 'Law' in all its human forms is a specialized slice of this more generalized normativity.

In Chapters 3 and 4 I will unfold these points more completely. However, some further philosophical backstory seems necessary, and this chapter provides an outline of some of its pertinent features. I will not attempt to cover everything of relevance, which would be impossible. Rather, I will sketch a selective and probably somewhat conventional narrative tracking elements from the history of ideas that are significant in the development of what is broadly understood as a process ontology of

DOI: 10.4324/9781003128335-3

nature. These ideas centre on the definition of 'nature', human and non-human, and the ongoing conflict between mechanistic and teleological accounts of the nonhuman.

Nature, in the Wider Sense

It may appear that the idea of 'nature' is outdated for theory, just as the idea of the 'environment' is problematic. Both terms conventionally refer to something other than the human sphere: the thing that we are not (or that we have transcended) and the space that surrounds us. This otherness is indicated by two of the *Oxford English Dictionary* definitions within the sub-category of 'senses relating to the material world':

11. a. The phenomena of the physical world collectively; esp. plants, animals, and other features and products of the earth itself, as opposed to humans and human creations.
    b. In wider sense: the whole natural world, including human beings; the cosmos. *Obsolete.*[1]

In its primary usage relating to external things, 'nature' refers collectively to the physical things of the Earth as opposed to human beings and human creations. The 'wider sense' of nature that includes human beings and the cosmos is marked as 'obsolete'. Since all life, including human life, consists of exchanges of matter between the organism and its habitat broadly construed, should terms that appear to sever humanity from its others be avoided or even abandoned? Latour says, '[e]cology clearly is not the irruption of nature into the public sphere but the *end of "nature"* as a concept that would allow us to sum up our relations to the world and pacify them'.[2] Even more strongly, he comments that 'for westerners and those who have imitated them, "nature" has made the world uninhabitable'.[3] At the same time, it is neither desirable nor possible to discard terms that are commonly used and invested with such rich meanings. Instead, it is necessary to have a good (if not exhaustive) understanding of the variability of meanings; to aim for as clear usage as is possible (bearing in mind that absolute clarity is an impossibility); and finally, to enhance those meanings that are constructive and prefigurative. Given the critique of a nature that is 'opposed' to human beings and the growing consciousness that we are in nature, perhaps

---

1 'Nature', *Oxford English Dictionary*, online version, April 2021.
2 Latour 2018, 36.
3 Ibid.

a more effective strategy than discarding 'nature' is to revive the obsolete meaning: 'the whole natural world, including human beings; the cosmos'.

The Physical World

The term 'nature' denotes several quite different things. Starting with spaces of 'nature' that are familiar to legal theory, nature is construed as external and/or internal to the human being. That 'nature' which is understood as outside the self,[4] external nature, is the singular physical world constructed by scientists, that is, physical reality as constituted by scientific knowledge. As the realm of fact, in post-Enlightenment science and philosophy singular physical nature has frequently been understood as non-normative and devoid of its own values. It is governed by physical laws and causal necessities and can be known objectively. Insistence on the facticity of external nature became one way of removing both God and the self from knowledge.[5] This approach contrasts with earlier ancient and medieval views in which the cosmos and its components were invested with a guiding purpose.

In keeping with the notion that nature was exterior to and separate from human selves, the tradition of jurisprudence side-lined physical nature as the mere acted upon of law (nature is that which is constituted, determined, coded, categorized, and so forth): law, by contrast is understood by the jurisprudential tradition as mental, abstract, and subsisting in the realm of ideas. Given the present state of theory and knowledge about the entanglement of mind and body and about the role that material things play in the narratives that underpin concepts, such a position is no longer plausible. Nor is it possible to exclude purpose from the nonhuman realm. Scientists are themselves no longer in agreement about the singularity of physical reality: a non-unified situation persists between the macro and the quantum scales, and at least one version of its resolution requires that we inhabit only one of many universes.[6] If we were not actually *in* one, that is, if we were outside everything that exists (an impossibility, of course), we would see a pluriverse. Scientists are also alive to the interference that observation makes[7] or,

---

4 The internal/external topography to describe the self and the world is itself a modern development. See Bordo 1986.
5 The elimination of God from natural philosophy was not immediate. Michael Forster 2019, s 11 says that in the eighteenth century 'German philosophy was still deeply committed to a sort of game of trying to reconcile the insights of the Enlightenment, especially those of modern natural science, with religion, and indeed more specifically with Christianity'.
6 Prigogine 1997.
7 Adopting the Kantian distinction between noumena and phenomena, cognitive scientist Donald Hoffman 2019 refers to the senses as an 'interface' with an inaccessible reality,

if not exactly 'interference' since this suggests some original state of affairs, then the determination or fixity that observation brings with it. Karen Barad says: 'Matter is never a settled matter. It is always radically open'.[8] And, perhaps most pertinently for my purposes here, the normativity of living beings (that they are characterized by self-generated and dynamic norms) now seems reasonably well established in biology.[9] The normativity of non-living things is less well established but, as I will explain in Chapter 4, the dense entanglements of life and nonlife, the formation of complex systems, and the directedness of earthly change provide some helpful scientific fodder for thinking about the normativity of nonliving processes.

In addition to the conceptualization of nature as *one* external physical space, there is also much now written about multiple natures or worlds associated with the many ways of becoming. This theory is a successor explanation to cultural relativism. Instead of simply perceiving *the* world differently, worlds are made and performed as different by different human agents but also by nonhuman beings, who engage in and create their own worlds.[10] The diversity of worlds may not yet be captured particularly well by mainstream thinking but is frequently deployed in disciplines such as anthropology. Ontological plurality is known variously through terms such as *multiverse, pluriverse,* or *fractiverse.*[11] These terms encapsulate heterogeneity in the present as well as the plural possibilities for world creation that exist among agential beings.

As a space construed as external therefore, nature is always nonetheless entangled with perception and practices of being. This is hardly surprising since we are part of nature, having evolved with it, and any separation from it is only ever conditional upon epistemic framing. But any effort to unpack nature as an external thing is also complicated by the persistent cultural

---

using the analogy of an icon on the computer desktop which is an interface with a software program. The senses are adapted for the survival of particular organisms (and thus vary significantly between species) rather than complete perception.

8 Barad 2012, 214.

9 Canguilhem 1966/1978; Nicholson 2018.

10 Lugones 1987 is an early exposition of ontological plurality as experience and being in different environments. Without using this terminology Lugones speaks of a co-becoming of the person and the world, but also of moving or travelling between worlds (which are never separate because they are occupied by agents who move between them). Lugones uses the language of perception and construction as well as making, experiencing, and doing – there appears to be no distinction in her analysis between ontology and epistemology.

11 See Mol 1998 (on ontological multiplicity); also Verran 2018 ('multiverse'); Law 2015 ('fractiverse'); De la Cadena and Blaser 2018; Law and Lien 2018. In the context of law, see Grabham 2016, ch 1.

resonances that the term and its various referents carry within the systems of meaning that have come to dominate human politics. I have already mentioned, for instance, the alignment of 'nature' with categories of socially marginalized groups. Whole categories of people have been discursively aligned with physical nature because they are thought to be basically part of it, like Indigenous peoples, or they are thought of as being somehow more embodied, such as women. Other groups, the more powerful, are associated with the valuable progress-enhancing aspects of human nature, notably an allegedly exclusive human capacity for reason. Based on prejudice about capacity and humanness, these stereotypes have a self-fulfilling trajectory in the present, with privilege aggregating around the persona of the white male more than any other group.

Immanent Being and Purpose

By contrast to understandings of physical nature as a spatial field external to the self, the sense of 'nature' that has more usually been extensively deployed and critiqued in legal and political theory is human nature. 'Human' nature could refer to the embodied living self but is more usually used to refer to the abstract and even purportedly essential properties or characteristics of human beings. 'Nature' in the context of natural law theory refers to an essence or inherent quality rather than to matter and the physical world. Human nature is said to be aligned with human goods and an objective and universal moral law that is said, by those who believe that such a thing exists, to provide a template or a guide for the design of human law. Attributions of content to this essence have been fraught by choices that arguably have as much to do with the politics and preferences of the commentator as they do with the diversity of human characteristics.

In addition to apparently 'external' physical reality, 'nature' therefore also applies to the essence of a thing. These senses are clearly connected, since physical things have properties that are used to describe and categorize them. The things of physical nature have natures. However, to speak in this way reveals another fracture in nature which is of critical significance to understanding the normativity of the natural world. Nature in the sense of an essence that is to be found within the things of physical nature often implies a teleological and – in science – highly controversial resonance. One of Aristotle's senses of nature was 'the primary immanent element in a thing, from which its growth proceeds'.[12] He viewed the nature of a thing to

---

12 Aristotle 1984a, 1602 (*Metaphysics* V, 4). See also 1984b, 330 (*Physics* II, 1).

be purposive, that is, directed towards an end and even a final state in which its immanent nature is fully realized.

The teleological rendition of nature was largely foreclosed by post-Enlightenment science with its insistence on the objectivity and facticity of the physical world and its often rigid fact-norm distinction. Science aimed to describe the regularities of the physical world and on the basis of those descriptions develop predictive theories that account for what does and will occur. Until recently, the dominant scientific narrative under the influence of Descartes has seen all of the material world, even all of life, as part of a giant machine that can be described and, with sufficient descriptive and theoretical detail, predicted.[13] As mentioned above, with the rise of biology and evolutionary theory, however, acceptance of the teleological proper-ties of life became unavoidable – clearly, biological processes and organ-isms have purposes.[14] The existence of purpose is not confined to single organisms (insofar as such a thing exists) but is also apparent in holobionts, superorganisms, collectives, hives, colonies, swarms, ecosystems, and so forth. Purposeful action may not be directed at a *final* end or state of perfec-tion, but action, movement, and behaviour are nonetheless oriented rather than random or disordered.

The term 'teleology' nonetheless remained controversial because of its anthropocentric and religious connotations: for instance, 'teleology' has been associated with the implication that there is an invisible 'vital force' (a god?) directing nonhuman life, an overall design and progress towards perfection, or the ability of a being to make a conscious choice.[15] None of these associations are, however, necessary to a 'teleological' nature.[16] The term *teleonomic* is sometimes used within biology and philosophy of biol-ogy as a contrast to *teleological*.[17] This term covers a range of perspectives: to capture purpose without Aristotelian final causation; to clarify that there is no intelligence behind the inbuilt design or agenda of organisms; and/or to

---

13 See eg Allen 2005; Turner 2013; see also essays collected in Garber and Roux 2013 and in Henning and Scarfe 2013.

14 See Grene 1974; Okrent 2017.

15 Mayr 1974.

16 Stephen Asma 2018, 20 comments that there 'are a few different teleology traditions, but the Anglo-American conversation has been blithely unaware of all but the dumbest and loudest version'.

17 *Nomos* = law, right; *logos* = word, ground. The variable meanings of these terms in ancient texts makes the attempt to distinguish teleonomy and teleology futile. See eg Zartaloudis 2019. The significant – and for some scientists objectionable – part of the terms is *telos* or function, purpose, which is the same regardless of whether it is attached to logos or nomos. See eg Hennig 2011; Lennox 1994.

reflect the Kantian point that biology needs language to speak of organisms *as if* they have purposes without conceding that they *do* have purposes.[18] Maturana and Varela, for instance, say their proposal that 'living systems are physical autopoietic machines' means that 'teleonomy becomes only an artifice of their description which does not reveal any feature of their organization'.[19] This view seems now to have receded under the weight of evidence and opinion that living things have their own purposes: they have mechanisms but are not mechanical. As mentioned in Chapter 1, many science theorists also now accept that there is a teleology inherent in the non-living world because of the inherent nature of energy to dissipate. Energy is teleological – and therefore normative – because it spreads. As Sagan and Margulis ask, 'Rather than thinking ourselves, along with Descartes, as rare aspects of the divine mind mulling about in a senselessly extended body, why should we not consider human purposefulness as rooted in the thermo-dynamic teleology of nature?'[20] Although such a suggestion may appear to reduce the living to the nonliving, and biology to physics, the physical laws in question – unlike those of Newton – are neither mechanical nor deterministic and hence cannot be used as a basis for the simple reduction of life to nonlife. I will explore this possibility in more detail in Chapter 4.

The remainder of this chapter adds more substance to some of the trajectories I have outlined, with specific reference to Aristotle's teleological assessment of nature and Kant's discussion of the tension between mechanistic and teleological accounts of organisms. These are the most influential classical philosophical sources used by bio-theory for understanding the teleologies of life and nonlife. Chapters 3 and 4 will take up the question of normativity in biological and nonliving nature.

Nature and the Human

It is not entirely correct to state (as I might have done in the past) that there is little 'nature' in natural law theory. Dennis des Chene says that 'as everyone knows' nature 'comes in two sizes: one size fits all, and extra large:'[21]

> The first, standardly glossed as 'essence' or 'quiddity', is that which defines each individual substance. . . . The second, glossed as 'world', 'universe', or 'cosmos', is the system of things which have natures in the first sense.

18 See Mayr 1974; Hennig 2011; Lennox 1994; Pross 2008.
19 Maturana and Varela 1980, 86.
20 Sagan and Margulis 2013, 226; cf Turner 2013.
21 Des Chene 1996, 212.

It is in the first sense – as essence or quiddity – that natural law purports to concern nature. The 'nature' in natural law, secular and not-so-secular, clearly consists of *human* nature or the 'natural properties of humans'.[22] 'Nature' in this context refers to an inherent quality or characteristic, rather than the physical world as a whole.[23] It is aligned with ancient ideas of nature as an intrinsic property and end of individuals rather than the 'extra large' physical contents of the entire world or cosmos.[24] The 'nature' of natural law is immanent, and not available to the senses. Thus, natural law of the jurisprudential tradition concerns what Kant called 'the moral law within' rather than the 'starry heavens above' (or anything in between).[25] Natural law is 'natural' because it purports to be about human nature and, importantly, the ends of human life – rationally adopted 'goods'. In its modern manifestations, natural law has little overt connection to broader concepts of nature that include the physical and living world. It is therefore discoverable by non-empirical methods such as the use of practical reason, rather than by observation and experimentation.

How natural law came to be about human nature rather than about nature more broadly is a complicated story. There are many philosophical, religious, and political transitions, from the ancient philosophers and especially Aristotle, via Aquinas and scholastic philosophy, through to the present. As my argument is not really about natural law theory, I will not discuss them all here. But several aspects of Aristotelianism remain of critical interest to contemporary discussions of nature and normativity – human and nonhuman – across all disciplines and are worth outlining. Most important is Aristotle's connection of nature to a final cause or end. Aristotle distinguished four different types of cause: the material (what something is made of); the formal (what form or shape it has); the efficient (the process by which it came to be that way); and the final (the purpose it serves).[26] In order to understand a thing completely, according to Aristotle, it is necessary to

22 Crowe 2019, 15. See also Chapter 1. There remains a sense in which there is little nature in natural law theory, since its claims about human nature are usually not substantiated by reference to any systematic or empirical study of nature, human or otherwise.

23 See *Oxford English Dictionary*, 'nature' III 'Senses relating to innate character' and IV 'Senses relating to the material world'.

24 See the discussion of the senses of nature in Des Chene 1996, 214–216.

25 Kant 1788/ 1993, 169.

26 Aristotle 1984b, 330 (*Physics*, Book II, 3). Leunissen 2010, 11 more precisely renders the causes as: '1) the "that out of which" . . . or the material cause; 2) the "what it is to be" . . . or the formal cause; 3) the that from which the origin of motion or rest comes" . . . or the efficient cause; 4) the "that for the sake of which" . . . or the final cause' (untranslated text and references to *Physics* omitted). See also Falcon 2019; Gotthelf 2012.

have an account of each of these causes. The most controversial by far for modern philosophy and science is the 'final' cause or 'that for the sake of which' – this is the idea that those final ends are embedded in the 'nature' of a thing and that knowledge of this nature is necessary to understand the thing in its states of rest and change. Change that follows nature is teleological, or responsive to the final end, which is embedded in it. There may be coincidences or accidents (such as when it rains in summer[27]) or changes that are motivated by something other than a thing's nature (the depression in the backyard did not appear from the soil's nature but because the dog dug a hole). However, when things unfold according to their immanent nature, their regularity is explained by their purpose:

> If then it is both by nature and for an end that the swallow makes its nest and the spider its web, and plants grow leaves for the sake of the fruit and send their roots down (not up) for the sake of nourishment, it is plain that this kind of cause is operative in things which come to be and are by nature. And since nature is twofold, the matter and the form, of which the latter is the end, and since all the rest is for the sake of the end, the form must be the cause in the sense of that for the sake of which.[28]

As Leunissen explains: 'Aristotle defines nature as an inner source of change and rest in that to which it belongs primarily of itself, and not accidentally'. By contrast artifacts 'require an external efficient cause – the art, hand, or tool of the artist – to become what they are'.[29] Nature is by definition normative: norms are immanent in things as their nature, and change and rest are responsive to these norms.

Some further pertinent aspects of Aristotle's teleology can be briefly noted. First, human and nonhuman life, and indeed the living and the nonliving, are in it together: the schema applies across the physical-material realm, though different objects and forms of life have different natures. Humans (those 'men' who are not slaves) are seen as by nature rational and political, and by virtue of these qualities different from other animals.[30] But in other respects we are just part of a broader sphere of animate and inanimate things that can be described and understood according to a set of common principles. Aristotle's *Physics* is not modern physics, which deals

---

27 Aristotle 1984b, 340 (*Physics*, II, 8).
28 Ibid.
29 Leunissen 2010, 16.
30 Aristotle 1997, 1253a1, 1253a7.

primarily with the interactions of matter as macro-objects and now, quantum objects – not only did Aristotle lay down principles for understanding everything composed of matter and subject to change; he considered the constitution of life as a process governed in part by the intrinsic nature of the living thing. Second, the *final* cause does not imply that the future causes the present or that the actual chronological end causes the beginning, though the beginning does lead by nature to that particular end, rather than some other. If everything goes according to 'nature' the potential of nature will be realized. But there are accidents and missteps, less perfect forms or adjacent forms that have their own distinct ends (women and slaves, for instance, are different by nature for Aristotle from free men). Nature as end is directive and explanatory but not chronologically last – there is no inverted chronology or ' "mysterious causal pull" from the future'.[31] Moreover, the final cause does not rely on any intention or design – some things have been designed to fulfil a purpose (such as a knife for cutting) but other things have an intrinsic purpose arising from their own nature.

Elements of Aristotelian thinking have become commonplace – often not helpfully – in modern thought. The idea, for instance, that human beings and other species are directed in some way by an intrinsic nature is fairly standard. This idea has been generalized and sometimes applied without any critique or evidence whatsoever to whole classes of things and people, leading to pernicious and entrenched distributions of social power.[32] This is not to cast doubt on genuinely biological factors that influence and constrain life. But, like nature as an object of perception, human nature has been culturally produced and then claimed to be part of nature: Lorraine Code comments that 'epistemology, like philosophy in general, has been in the business of naturalizing as it goes'.[33] Whilst pretending to be grounded in human nature, various fields of philosophy have instead 'naturalize[d] the very attributes and actions that they purport to discover'.[34] Aristotle himself notoriously defended both slavery and the female-male hierarchy on the grounds of what he claimed were the natural properties of classes of people.[35] Such unsubstantiated essentialist-normative notions about human life and society have persisted across centuries in European thought and, despite continuing efforts to correct them, continue to affect social behaviour and judgement. The notion that natural change is directed towards a

31 Leunissen 2010, 8.
32 Code 1996; Plumwood 1993, 46–47; cf Allchin and Werth 2020.
33 Code 1996, 6.
34 Ibid.
35 Aristotle 1997, 1252a34; see discussion by Plumwood 1993, 46–47.

final state, reborn in the Enlightenment as an ideology of progress associated primarily with human life and European culture, remains influential.

Despite problematic uses of the Aristotelian scheme, there are elements of the idea that change in the physical world is purposive that remain helpful for understanding the normativity of nature. After all, as Mark Okrent has commented: 'teleological discourse is inherently normative'.[36] But the 'end' of teleology is not necessarily a final state, or an immanent nature imagined as potential for full realization of that nature: the 'end' might simply be the next step in maintaining life while the norm is the process the organism establishes or follows in order to pursue that inherent end. Teleology can simply suggest a moment-to-moment directional unfolding of a process.[37]

Teleological Life

In the transition to modernity, the normative, essentialist, and teleological aspects of nature were narrowed to *human* nature and, in particular, the human as a rational being capable of consciously pursuing their own purposes. This narrowing of normative nature to human essence, and in particular to our apparently 'natural' capacity for reason, formed the basis for much of the political, moral, and legal philosophy of recent centuries. It was accompanied by a devaluation and disenchantment, or what Val Plumwood calls 'backgrounding', of physical nonhuman nature.[38] Descartes, for instance, viewed the nonhuman living world as mechanical rather than purposive because it was composed entirely of *res extensa*, extended matter, rather than unextended *res cogitans*, or thought.[39] Dennis Des Chene points out that Descartes' characterization of nature as mechanical was not universally adopted as an *ontology* of the nonhuman but that nonetheless more modest mechanical *explanations* of the natural world were widely adopted in post-Cartesian philosophy and science:[40] 'Mechanism as ontology failed but mechanism as method succeeded'.[41] In other words, whether or not

36 Okrent 2017, 99.
37 Sagan and Margulis 2013, 225 write 'As Aristotle intuited, there is a prevailing, inherent, not-necessarily-conscious *telos* or entelechy – an internal *telos* – that is natural. And this naturalistic teleology is genuinely retrocausal without being supernatural'.
38 Plumwood 1993, 21.
39 On Cartesian dualism see, eg Descartes 1982/1644, Part I: ss8–11; Plumwood 1993, 104.
40 Des Chene 2005. Garland Allen 2005 makes a similar distinction between philosophical and operative mechanisms among biologists and philosophers of biology of the late eighteenth and early nineteenth centuries.
41 Des Chene 2005, 249.

animals have souls, consciousness, and can 'think', biological processes, and matter at large, could still be explained in mechanical terms.[42] Such a view across the living world seems to have dominated biology until the twentieth century and continues to be influential, though in increasingly complex and non-reductive forms.[43] Another aspect of Descartes' dualistic scheme that resonated spectacularly throughout culture more generally was what Susan Bordo (following Karl Stern) calls the 'masculinization of thought'; the downgrading of the earth and its generativity to mechanism, the insistence on an individuated and interior self, and the prominence given to rationality as the cure for doubt that arises from sensory engagements.[44]

Organisms were, however, widely regarded as posing a philosophical problem for mechanistic ontologies of the nonhuman world because, by all appearances, they did not themselves follow mechanistic laws but appeared to be incalculable in form and behaviour. Anton Kabeshkin provides a roadmap of five different approaches to this perceived contradiction that existed by the end of the eighteenth century.[45] A quick overview will help to understand the different positions regarding mechanism and vitalism that followed this critical period in the western philosophy of nature. The first approach was reductive – that organisms *could* be explained entirely in materialistic terms by reference to the predictable laws of physics and chemistry but, as they are so complex, further scientific progress was needed to get to this stage. The second 'vitalist' approach was that organisms had a *non*-material 'vital force' or 'formative drive' – in German known as *Bildungstrieb*.[46] This has the benefit of some kind of explanation (even if it still begs the question of what the vital force actually is) though scientists and radical materialists are sceptical of any ontology that requires a metaphysical (*super*natural) element. A third approach was also vitalist but pragmatic rather than metaphysical, using the idea of vital force as an interpretive placeholder that would suffice until more accurate scientific analysis was conducted, the assumption being that knowledge would over time improve to facilitate this. The fourth position was advanced by Kant: I describe it in more detail below, but it essentially came to the view that, whilst organisms

---

42 Mechanical theory of the early modern period is normally characterized by its opposition to Aristotle's depiction of a teleological nature. However, such a characterization simplifies a complex history. See generally, essays collected in Garber and Roux 2013.
43 Woese 2004; Glennan 2010; see generally Glennan and Illari 2018; Garber and Roux 2013; Dupré 2013.
44 Bordo 1986.
45 Kabeshkin 2017, 1183–1187.
46 See also Bennett 2010, 65.

appear to contradict mechanism, the limits of human understanding mean that we can only ever regard this as an appearance. The final approach, that of Schelling, is described by Kabeshkin in terms that indicate a bypassing of the reductive-vitalist distinction and arguably brings him into closer alignment with the biophilosophy of the early twentieth century and even modern process biology. Schelling emphasized the complexity of organic systems, the precedence of production to product, the internal-external processing of matter, the need for ongoing self-maintenance in the face of external irritants, and the situatedness of human beings in the natural world.[47] These characteristics of life render unnecessary the idea of a metaphysical vital force and at the same time show that life cannot be reduced to mechanical and predictable laws.

Schelling's naturephilosophy[48] is extremely suggestive and more resonant with contemporary theory than Kant's. I will have a little more to say about it at the end of this chapter. However, Kant is important, especially in relation to norms and normativity, because his emphasis on teleology laid bare a philosophical problem that has defined later analysis. Kant completely accepted the mechanistic view of nature but was also clearly troubled by the apparent non-mechanical nature of living things. (I note but cannot here consider properly controversy about how Kant's racism is connected to his critical philosophy and in particular to the *Critique of Judgement*, in which, according to Cassirer, Kant 'spoke as the logician for Linneaus' descriptive [and taxonomical] science'.[49]) In Part II of the *Critique of Judgement*, the 'Critique of Teleological Judgement', Kant directly addressed the purposive aspects of living things: '[o]rganisms are . . . the only beings in nature that, considered in their separate existence and apart from any relation to other things, cannot be thought possible except as ends of nature'.[50] A natural end is one that is 'both cause and effect of itself'.[51] He provided the example of a tree, which reproduces itself as another tree, which grows, and which has parts that maintain the whole.[52] As Angela Breitenbach says, the news that organisms have natural purposes 'comes as a bit of a surprise' because

47 Schelling 1799/2004; Kabeshkin 2017, 1188–1199.
48 The term is used by Iain Grant 2006. Many commentators use the German term *Naturphilosophie* to refer to this particular school of thought in German idealism.
49 Quoted in Sandford 2018, 958. Bernasconi 2003 makes many compelling points about why the racism of European philosophers should not be excised from a consideration of their philosophy.
50 Kant 1790/1952, §65, 376.
51 Ibid, §64, 371.
52 Ibid, §64, 371–372.

it sits uneasily with the causally driven account of nature in the *Critique of Pure Reason*.[53] Kant set out an antinomy in the *Critique of Judgement* to capture the problem that nature requires mechanical explanation but that organisms elude such explanation. The form of the antinomy is relatively straightforward:[54] first, that mechanical laws are necessary to explain everything in nature; but second that some things, in particular 'organized beings' (ie organisms), cannot be explained mechanically because they appear to be their own cause and effect, both final causes and purposes.[55] Kant underlined the impossibility of understanding living entities mechanically in what has become a famous passage, where he noted the absurdity of thinking that there will ever be a Newton to explain a blade of grass:

> It is, I mean, quite certain that we can never get a sufficient knowledge of organized beings and their inner possibility, much less get an explanation of them, by looking merely to mechanical principles of nature. Indeed, so certain is it, that we may confidently assert that it is absurd for men even to entertain any thought of so doing or to hope that maybe another Newton may some day arise, to make intelligible to us even the genesis of but a blade of grass from natural laws that no design has ordered. Such insight we must absolutely deny to mankind.[56]

The claim that there can never be a *Newton* to explain life *may* remain good, despite over two centuries of advances in biology since Kant wrote the third critique in 1790, including the fundamental advances of Darwinism. If Kant meant that life cannot have an explicator as good as Newton was for physical interactions, he was arguably wrong. But if he meant (as seems more likely given the mechanical models of his time) that life cannot be reduced to mechanical explanations of the type that Newton delivered for physics, he was almost certainly right.[57] Scientists now have a much

---

53 Breitenbach 2008, 351. See also comments by Ginsborg 2019, s 3.4 that some interpretations of what Kant means by 'mechanism' in the third critique make his solution to the antinomy 'radically at odds' with parts of the first critique.

54 In fact, there are two versions of the antinomy, as Breitenbach 2008, 351 points out – one which is about the world itself and the other about how we understand the world.

55 Kant 1790/1952, §70, 387. In Aristotelian terms the distinction is between things that can be explained only by reference to 'efficient causes', that is, by the interaction of material things that produces effects and 'final causes' or inbuilt purposes.

56 Ibid, §75, 400.

57 Kauffman 2013, 6 argues that Kant was right on the basis that '[n]o laws entail the evolution of the biosphere'. The critical concept here is *entail*, which implies determinism. This does not preclude non-deterministic laws from being involved in the generation of life.

clearer picture of many of the 'mechanical' components of life, including its biochemistry and biophysics, and the conditions that over many millions of years may have allowed forms of life to accrue from nonlife. Nonetheless, there is not, and probably never will be, a 'mechanical' understanding of life; first because life works on probabilities and pathways rather than necessities, and second because in life mechanics gives way to the self-generated norms of adaptation and survival. 'Design' is built into life as the product of eons of evolutionary change brought about by natural selection and other processes, not ordered from outside. This is not to say that there are no mechanical aspects of life (there may be many, depending on how 'mechanical' is interpreted) or that it didn't start via some mechanism, if not mechanically (it may have, though Kant thought not). Kant's claim might now be rewritten: despite (and because of) the intricate complexity of the mechanics of life and the fact that these intersecting complexities generate probable rather than necessary effects, they resolve into something that can never be mechanically explained. That is, although there are multiple intersecting mechanical parts to life, the sum of these parts remains qualitatively different from the entirely contingent forms that nonliving physical entities take.

The antinomy between mechanical and purposive or teleological explanations of life is important because of the normative implications of teleology.[58] There are many discussions of the antimony and proposed solutions[59] which, though important, are more intricate than I can consider here. One view that has relevance for law is that the apparent purpose of an organism provides an invitation to judge whether it is behaving as it ought, following its own norms. Hannah Ginsborg argues that the solution to the antinomy lies in the normative quality of judgements about living things.[60] There are many steps in her intricate argument, but the critical point is that the claim that organisms are (and have) purposes provides criteria for normative judgements that are made about them, for instance in scientific investigations. A teleological judgement is about assessing whether the organism does or becomes what it is supposed to do or be:

> The regularity with which an acorn grows into an oak or a heart circulates blood, is lawlike in so far as these processes conform to laws saying that acorns ought to (are meant to, are supposed to) grow into oaks or that the heart ought to circulate blood. Regarding organic regularities

58 See generally Okrent 2017.
59 In particular see Breitenbach 2008; Ginsborg 2001; Allison 1991.
60 Ginsborg 2001.

as lawlike in this way requires that we regard organisms and their parts as subject to normative standards or constraints: and this is just what it is to regard them as purposes.[61]

In other words, the purposes of living nature feed into the process of making judgements about nature – we must regard the organism *as if* it had a purpose and as law*like* in order to understand and judge it.[62] The organism itself is inscrutable and its normativity is rolled into the process of human judgement. The upshot of this argument is that, even though all organisms seem to have purposes and are their own designers, only for *human* beings does this have any normative consequences: it gives us the criteria by which to judge organisms. Law and normativity belong to the sphere of human judgement while organisms – and the entirety of nature – remain inscrutable.

It is true of course that we can't know whether other creatures exercise teleological judgement and what it looks like,[63] just as it is technically true that there is an element of solipsism to all human experience and knowledge. But Kant's analysis leaves western philosophy far short of a comprehension that organisms – and the Earth as a system of systems – have any self-directed constitutive normativity.[64] Nonhuman life remains in the realm of object to the human knowing subject. By contrast, as mentioned above, Friedrich Schelling argued that it was not only legitimate but necessary to see purpose as intrinsic to organisms, rather than just as a category used to describe them. Regardless of the fact that thinking of organisms as purposive entities is a construct of human judgement, Schelling argued that we don't have any choice about thinking in this way: 'the purposiveness of natural products dwells in *themselves*, . . . it is *objective* and *real*, hence . . . it belongs, not to your *arbitrary*, but to your *necessary* representations'.[65]

Life then, for Schelling, could be regarded as intrinsically teleological, not just apparently so. He saw clearly that the separation of nature from the

---

61 Ibid, 252.
62 See also Kauffmann 2013, 4 (discussing Monod's view about the apparent purposes of certain organisms – 'a mere "as if" teleology'); Sandford 2018.
63 For instance, we can't know what the experience of intending something might be for a dog. Kant evidently thought purpose was necessarily intentional: see van den Berg 2014, 90.
64 There is much more that could be said on the question of Kant's views on life. For a particularly fascinating commentary that challenges any simplistically dualistic account, see Caygill 2007.
65 Schelling 1797/1989, 32.

human, in particular from the 'I', led to its objectification and an inability to see it as alive:

> So long as I myself am *identical* with Nature, I understand what a living nature is as well as I understand my own life; I apprehend how this universal life of Nature reveals itself in manifold forms, in progressive developments, in gradual approximations to freedom. As soon, however, as I separate myself, and with me everything ideal from Nature, nothing remains to me but a dead object, and I cease to comprehend how a life outside me can be possible.[66]

Insisting on the human-nonhuman, subject-object, separation leads to an emphasis on products rather than productivity. In objectifying and categorizing everything, we fail to pay attention to the productive process that always pre-exists any product. Schelling used the example of an impeded stream – later also used by Cuvier and by Woese at the turn of the twenty-first century[67] – to illustrate the flow of nature and the quality of its (always temporary) objects:

> *Example*: a stream flows in a straight line forward as long as it encounters no resistance. Where there is resistance – a whirlpool forms. Every original product of nature is such a whirlpool, every organism. The whirlpool is not something immobilized, it is rather something constantly transforming – but reproduced anew at each moment. Thus no product in nature is *fixed*, but it is reproduced at each instant through the force of nature entire.[68]

Schelling went on to argue that there are 'infinitely many points of inhibition' that break up the stream of nature's productivity, resulting in the many products of nature we see around us. But behind it all 'Nature is originally pure identity – nothing to be distinguished in it'.[69] He therefore elaborated what looks, to modern eyes, a kind of process philosophy, emphasizing action, motion, becoming, and production over the entities or products of nature.

Schelling's natural philosophy suffered in part because of 'largely indefensible' empirical claims[70] and 'outdated scientific theories'.[71] It has also,

---

66 Ibid, 36.
67 Cuvier, quoted in Nicholson 2018, 149; Woese 2004, 176.
68 Schelling 1799/2004, 18.
69 Ibid.
70 Bowie 2020, 1.
71 Kabeshkin 2017, 1180.

at least in Anglophone philosophy, been sidelined in favour of better-known philosophical names. Despite the extensive critique by nineteenth-century scientists, Schelling's naturephilosophy has much in common with process philosophy. The decline in popularity of mechanistic-reductive-objective world views among science philosophers, and in particular bio-theorists, in favour of more process-oriented and ecological accounts has led to a revival of interest in Schelling (admittedly still in its early stages).[72] In thinking about law and normativity, the difference between Kant and Schelling is stark. For Kant, despite the *apparently* purposive quality of organisms, normativity belongs entirely in the human sphere as a human construct. For Schelling, on the other hand, regardless of the limitations of human cognition, we are *forced* to see that organisms – and natural things in general – are purposive because we can't see them any other way. Hence the antinomy framed by Kant has – if Schelling's account is accepted[73] – been resolved to the extent that purpose, and hence directedness and normativity, are inherent in nature.

Conclusion

The nature that has for the past several centuries informed the form and content of law has mostly been understood as essential *human* nature, while physical nature has been relegated to the status of an external object of law generally assumed to be non-normative. The paradigm change now unfolding promotes an active, process-oriented view of physical nature – this transition in natural philosophy is built partly upon the excavation of countertraditions in western thought to do with process ontology, vitalism, and teleology, and partly upon modern scientific re-evaluation of the metaphysics of nature.[74] The tide has turned against mechanistic ontology in science. Although it might be thought that mechanism is already long dead in the social sciences, the anti-mechanistic and process-oriented science theory of recent decades provides vast resources for new philosophizing that is materialist but neither reductive nor reliant on a non-material vitality. Vitality exists, of course, but it emerges from within the complex relations and flows of materiality. There is no longer any rationale for maintaining faith in the mechanistic character of life (or even of nonlife) and it is possible to say that

---

72　See, for instance, the special edition of *Rivista di estetica* 2020, volume 74: 'Rethinking Schelling: Nature, Myth, Realism'.
73　I clearly can't offer an assessment of the whole system. But see Kabeshkin 2017; Lauer 2012, 33–55; Peterson 2004; Bowie 2020.
74　See eg Nicholson and Dupré 2018; Henning and Scarfe 2013.

the purposive character of organized beings, of all life, makes them normative in themselves (not only in how we judge them). That is, organisms live
according to norms that are emergent, not the determined cause and effect of
machines. As I will explain in the next chapter, the vital normativity of life
was theorized by Canguilhem as an emergent inherent property of organisms: for Canguilhem, normativity is not about judgement or knowledge but
about the existence and persistence of the living organism.

3 Biogenesis and Jurisgenesis

Introduction

Aristotle, Kant, and Schelling shed different kinds of light on the history and theory of the nature-law/normativity relationship. Aristotle is significant because of his view that things, including humans, have an intrinsic nature that is teleological and normative. Many centuries later, Kant argued that, as purposes, organisms appear to be an exception to the otherwise mechanical causation in the universe. But Kant did not reject mechanism. For Kant, understanding natural purposes requires the development of teleological judgement, the upshot of which is that to understand life we judge it normatively, that is, according to assumed purposes. By contrast, Schelling has been marginalized in Anglophonic histories of philosophy but was influential in the early development of biology and biophilosophy. Like Nietzsche, he placed the human being inside nature and accepted the intrinsic teleology of life.

In this chapter I continue these reflections by turning to Georges Canguilhem whose thought about vital normativity contains elements of both Aristotle and Kant but is tied to neither. Canguilhem situated normativity not in the essence of an entity or in its universal character or, like Kant, within the horizon of human judgement, but in the immanent biological processes that constitute *living* and maintaining life. Canguilhem is little studied in Anglophonic legal theory,[1] but his thought is helpful in the development of a materialist and ecologically directed account of law. Canguilhem's work on vital normativity is highly suggestive and can be extended towards a socio-ecological reading. His focus on the organism means that the wider norm-producing processes of ecosystems remained nascent but open for consideration. Further, he distinguished between the normative qualities of

---

1 Though he is not entirely unknown; see eg Pottage 2015.

DOI: 10.4324/9781003128335-4

organisms and those of society, while leaving room for developing both parallels and continuities between them. The arguably 'biochauvinist'[2] character of Canguilhem's work means that in his work the continuities between living and nonliving normativity are underexplored.

New Normals and New Natures: Canguilhem on Vital Normativity

Humans, like all animals and all life, are co-emergent with their habitat and subsist according to a normativity that is immanent to life. It seems a banal truth to say that life follows norms and that these norms first arise from the emergence and development of life itself. Georges Canguilhem said that 'life is in fact a normative activity'.[3] But it is more difficult to understand in theoretical terms the specific normative qualities of life and in particular *how* norms emerge, what material forms they take, what constitutes following them, how they change, and how they connect to human social norms and to our practices of law.

Many of these questions are addressed in Canguilhem's major work, *The Normal and the Pathological*, which was (for the most part) his doctorate in the philosophy of medicine in which he examined normative biological processes.[4] In speaking of life as normative, he was referring to the ways in which life is creative and establishes norms – an organism does not create just any norms, but norms that promote its own existence and that avoid suffering. 'Vital normativity' is the normativity embedded in biological processes and that is necessary to the continuation and reproduction of life. Life is not indifferent to its own existence but seeks to preserve it and hence to create norms that will promote life. 'Even for an amoeba, living means preference and exclusion'.[5] The same might even be said of a virus, even though it is on the edge of life in that it cannot survive and reproduce autonomously: it is nonetheless clearly driven to occupy living hosts and replicate within them.

Canguilhem repeatedly referred to 'the dynamic polarity of life' or embedded polar tendencies within living processes. Polarities are differences within a process or entity that are not separated or exclusive, but rather related by tension, in particular by attraction and repulsion: 'The

---

2 Wolfe 2015.

3 Canguilhem 1966/1978, 70.

4 The third part of the book was written in the 1960s and contains reflections on the first sections, as well as a number of important additions and developments.

5 Canguilhem 1966/1978, 76.

simplest biological nutritive system of assimilation and excretion expresses a polarity'.[6] The polarity that most defines Canguilhem's work is the polarity between the normal and the pathological, which is connected to – but does not entirely align with – the polarity of health and disease.[7] Canguilhem was insistent that the normal and the pathological are not essential states that can be ascribed by the scientist to an organism: they are not just statistical convergence and divergence. Rather, the normal emerges from vital normativity: it is the process through which the body or organism lives. More specifically, the organism repulses that which is of negative value but accepts that which does not cause pain and/or is adaptive: the organism thereby creates and lives by its own norms. Pathology or disease is not just difference from a prior state of normality but exists where a diversion from the norm is resisted by the organism: 'diversity is not disease: the *anomalous* is not the pathological. Pathological implies pathos, the direct and concrete feeling of suffering and impotence, the feeling of life gone wrong'.[8]

The *feeling* of negative value is the pathology: we might suppose that this ordinarily does align with the scientist's observation of things that are anomalous about an organism, but that is not necessarily the case. And hence the norm is not a statistical or objectively measured matter, but rather a value established by the organism. Vital normativity embeds values in the facts of living. This means, for instance, that a doctor's job is not to impose a normality as scientifically measured on the body, but rather to assist or 'extend' the body's own struggle against, or rejection of, negative values: 'It is life itself and not medical judgement which makes the biological normal a concept of value and not a concept of statistical reality'.[9] Just as selection of the most adapted traits is a natural process that can be accelerated by human intervention, so medicine is a natural process that can be enhanced by human knowledge and technology.[10]

It is this built-in assertion of life's own values, that is, the self-attributed value of living forms, that leads to the creation of new norms. An anomaly experienced by an organism is not of itself pathological because it might be functional or adaptive: it might be useful. Mutations and variations can mean that the organism, and then the species, become better suited to their

---

6 Ibid, 71.

7 There are numerous complexities in the discussion, for instance, in Canguilhem's observation that it is not normal to be healthy.

8 Canguilhem 1966/1978, 77; see further Talcott 2019.

9 Canguilhem 1966/1978, 73.

10 Ibid, 71–72, quoting Guyenot: 'The organism is an incomparable chemist. It is the first among physicians'.

environment. In consequence, 'normality' is a quality of neither the organism nor the environment but of both together:

> The species is the grouping of individuals, all of whom are different to some degree, whose unity expresses the momentary normalization of their relations with the environment, including other species, as Darwin had clearly seen. Taken separately, the living being and his environment are not normal: it is their relationship that makes them such. . . . A living being is normal in any environment insofar as it is the morphological and functional solution found by life as a response to the demands of the environment.[11]

Here, we see a recognition that norms and normality are relational rather than properties of individual beings or of environments. Both context and organism are composed of mutable norms: 'Because the qualified living being lives in a world of qualified objects, he lives in a world of possible accidents'.[12] Canguilhem rejected both the idea that an environment is a product of fixed and invariant physical and chemical laws and, on the other hand, merely random and meaningless: 'Nothing happens by chance, everything happens in the form of events. Here is how the environment is inconstant. Its inconstancy is simply its becoming, its history'.[13]

And hence, like human social existence, life does not go backwards. It is irreversible, cumulative, and historical: 'To be cured is to be given new norms of life, sometimes superior to the old ones. There is an irreversibility to biological normativity'.[14] For life, at least, the arrow of time moves inexorably forwards: this is not to suggest that there is progress towards perfection or some built-in end point,[15] but simply that there is always change and always movement building upon the past. This movement responds to a prior situation but does not perfectly reproduce it. Like the common law, changes aggregate rather than progress rationally, they pile up in records

---

11 Ibid, 81–82.
12 Ibid, 116.
13 Ibid, 116.
14 Ibid, 137.
15 Cf Darwin 1859/1906, 669: 'And as natural selection works solely by and for the good of each being, all corporeal and mental endowment will tend to progress towards perfection'. If, in Darwin's view, changes *tend* towards perfection, they do not necessarily reach it: 'Natural selection will not necessarily produce absolute perfection; nor, as far as we can judge by our limited faculties, can absolute perfection be everywhere predicated': Ibid, 260.

and traces, for instance as contained in the organism's own DNA, in its observable characteristics, and by extension in its ecosystem. Despite the 'qualified' character of both organism and environment and the relational nature of the normality that emerges between them, Canguilhem's discussion of biological normativity centres on the norms that single organisms create rather than those produced by groups or by interactions between a multitude of norm-producing agents of different species. Unsurprisingly, given the era in which *The Normal and the Pathological* was written, Canguilhem's dominant image of the environment remains a container or context to which the organism adapts in response to environmental change. For humans, this includes the historical-cultural society within which we are each placed: as Monica Greco says, for Canguilhem, 'human beings – *as the sort of organism they are* – are exceptionally open to social moulding and specifically required to function in a meaning-laden cultural environment'.[16] But he does not foreground or develop in detail a strongly ecological account of the complexity of interdependencies and co-constitutions that would situate norms as products of ecosystems as well as of individualizable entities. Hence vital normativity for Canguilhem is primarily something that attaches to organisms rather than arising within the complexities of ecosystems (or other systems).

Canguilhem rejected any simple analogizing between the norms of organisms and those of society as a whole.[17] Vital norms are immanent to an organism and produced out of the need for life to continue in a particular way. Vital norms are not chosen or imposed; they are 'presented without being represented, acting with neither deliberation nor calculation'.[18] Society also, arguably, has immanent needs and purposes that are the product of geographical and historical-cultural circumstances. But in addition to these historical norms, society designs itself intentionally – for instance via state law and regulation. Society consists of norms that are a combination of processes that are internal and self-regulative and imposed after reflection.[19] Society is 'both machine and organism'.[20] As I have indicated in earlier chapters, this lack of analogy between the organism and society does not imply that human law and nature are separate. Rather the law-nature assemblage is produced from intersecting biosocial normativities that include

16 Greco 1998, 242, emphasis in original.
17 Canguilhem 1966/1978, 154, 1965/2008, 72 ('Aspects of Vitalism'); Genel 2021.
18 Canguilhem 1966/1978, 154.
19 See generally Genel 2021.
20 Canguilhem 1966/1978, 155.

immanent natural norms, meaning-making world construction, and deliberative collective practices.

Canguilhem's discussion of normalization is a predecessor to various well-known theoretical moves of the later twentieth century.[21] It is reflected, for instance, in similar thinking that Foucault developed at the level of sociology and history. In *Madness and Civilization* Foucault suggested that the 'normal' of Enlightenment reason was produced in tandem with the expulsion of those regarded as insane and undesirable.[22] Writ large, this is reminiscent of Canguilhem's account of normativity as the result of an organism's avoidance of its own subjectively felt pain or discomfort. In both cases, the normal is the result of a process of normalization taking the form of the exclusion of a subjectively determined pathology: for Canguilhem the pathology is felt by the organism; for Foucault it is the result of disciplinary socio-political constructs and preferences.[23]

Sebastian Rand suggests that Canguilhem's work anticipated Derrida's analysis in 'Force of Law' which has been so much discussed in legal theory.[24] Rather than a 'straightforward' account of normativity in which norms are first created and then followed, Rand characterizes Canguilhem's analysis as producing a 'future-anterior temporality of normativity':[25] that is, the norm is produced in the process of following it and is retrospectively viewed, or felt, as having always-already been in existence. But Canguilhem's account of normativity is arguably also quite close to Derrida's discussions of repetition, law, and iterability in relation to signification. For Derrida 'law is always a law of repetition, and repetition is always submission to a law'.[26] Otherness is implied in the structure of law for Derrida – it is always immanent in any possible or actual repetition, for instance of a sign: any repetition is always an other to its 'original' since it is differentiated in time and always contains the possibility of inexactitude of context, of usage, of space, and so forth.[27] The 'original' (law, sign, idea) contains

21 See eg Genel 2021.
22 Foucault 1967.
23 Genel 2021. In the addition to *The Normal and the Pathological*, Canguilhem 1966/1978, 149 described generalized normality in the following way:

> The normal is the effect obtained by the execution of the normative project, it is the norm exhibited in the fact. In the relationship of the fact there is then a relationship of exclusion between the normal and the abnormal.

24 Rand 2011, 350.
25 Ibid.
26 Derrida 1981a, 123 ('Plato's Pharmacy').
27 'For the structure of iteration . . . implies both identity and difference. Iteration in its "purest form" – and it is always impure – contains in itself the discrepancy of a difference that constitutes it as iteration'. Derrida 1988, 53.

this otherness as part of its identity. This is the condition of repeatability, or iterability. Canguilhem's account of biological normativity also bears a resemblance to accounts of performativity that emphasize the mobility or emergence of performed identity as both a response to the past (action within constraints) and creative of the present and future.[28]

In an adjacent field, Canguilhem's thought can also be compared with a broader process ontology in which entities are emergent rather than stable, essential, or fixed.[29] The normative process is built into life; there is no existence without it and it is a process of inherent change and adaptation to circumstances. In legal theory, there is a much older analogue than Foucault, Derrida, or even process ontologies for Canguilhem's analysis of normativity: at the height of its development, the common law was regarded as the law of the land (ie England and Wales) that was always being made – established for a very long time but not fixed, and sometimes declared by judges as having existed in the fabric of the law even though not actually specified as such.[30] A judge is the 'mouthpiece' of the law rather than its inventor – constituted within law's process as much as participating in it. For the classical common law (if less so now), 'a norm cannot be original. Rule begins to rule only in making rules and this function of correction arises from infraction itself'.[31]

Canguilhem's analysis of vital normativity is significant because it locates the process of norm creation in the individual organism and, by extension, in the development of groups of organisms and ecosystems. It provides one persuasive account of emergent normativity; how norms are created and followed in biological processes. The same story works whether we are talking about an amoeba or an elephant. It also works for complex ecological relationships because organisms relating to each other and to habitat adjust their normative responses dynamically. Normality is therefore a process rather than a state of affairs, and the norms of nature are in constant revision.

Self, Norm, and World-Creating Agents

For Canguilhem, the norms of nature emerge from the polarity of normal and pathological, from the effort the organism makes to repair itself and avoid suffering, and from the dynamics of adaptation. The process of living

---

28 Butler 1990.
29 Grosz 2004 (discussing Darwin, Nietzsche, and Bergson); for an analytical philosophy version see Bickhard 2004.
30 Hale 1778/1971. On the distinction between the common law as 'general custom' and localized customs, see also Duxbury 2017, 342–343.
31 Canguilhem 1966/1978, 147. See also Lyotard and Thébaud 1985, 32–33.

involves a preference to expel suffering. The organism's life is therefore directed in some way rather than random: the process of life is purposive and teleological. The directed nature of life does not imply that there is intentional or conscious choice towards a particular goal, and nor does it imply a final state of being, or even progress towards perfection. There are no design principles that explain the organism's end apart from its preference to avoid suffering and to continue – its *conatus*. Rather, life's directedness simply implies that the immanent norms created by life are aligned with a purpose. As Mark Okrent has put it, 'Taken as a whole, the life processes of an organism are for the sake of continuing those life processes; the goal of a living thing is to continue to be the living thing that it is'.[32]

Canguilhem's emphasis on subjective preference provides one angle on living agency that is biological and normative rather than mechanical and reactive. The experience of subjectivity, that is, of having an internal perspective vis-à-vis an external world, was also explored by biophilosophers of the early twentieth century. For instance, Helmuth Plessner argued that the defining characteristics of organisms are that they have both boundary and positionality.[33] From the outside, a boundary locates an organism in space. From the inside, a boundary locates the bodily limit of our unfolding life and thus an experience of our self. A rock has a boundary that places its form in space and time, but only a *life* form has a boundary which is part of its identity and self-experience.[34] Like all boundaries, the boundary of a living thing is not just a meaningless limit, but is ontologically complex: permeable, relational, and given meanings by the self and by others.

Jakob von Uexküll, also imagining the interiority of life,[35] considered each organism to have an *Umwelt* – a self-created meaningful environment or bubble. In his *Foray into the Worlds of Animals and Humans*, he invited his readers to take a stroll with him:

> We begin such a stroll on a sunny day before a flowering meadow in which insects buzz and butterflies flutter, and we make a bubble around each of the animals living in the meadow. The bubble represents each animal's environment [*Umwelt*] and contains all the features accessible to the subject. As soon as we enter into one such bubble, the previous

32 Okrent 2017, 97.
33 Plessner 1928/2019, ch 4.
34 Grene 1974, 323 (a nonliving object 'fills space' while a living being '*takes* its place'); see also 324–325; Plessner 1928/2019, 84, 93; Bernstein 2019, xlvi–lii.
35 Canguilhem wrote about Uexküll in 'The Living and Its Milieu': Canguilhem 1965/2008; see Pottage 2015.

surroundings of the subject are completely reconfigured. Many qualities of the colorful meadow vanish completely, others lose their coherence with one another, and new connections are created. A new world arises in each bubble.[36]

In its essence, this bubble, or *Umwelt*, is an extension of Kant's view that space and time are produced by the 'unity of apperception' through which 'different qualities are constantly being associated into unities'.[37] Uexküll pointed out that – because of varying perceptual capabilities and abilities to act on the environment – the bubble around animals is different from that around humans and, therefore, biologists need to take a distinctive approach to understanding animal spacetime: the biologist 'cannot do as the physicist, i.e. regard the space of human beings as the only reality and, without more ado, transplant animals into that'.[38] Rather, the biologist 'must make a detailed inquiry concerning the factors from which the space is composed where lives the particular animal'.[39] Uexküll argued that this work of particularizing the spacetime bubble of the organism could be understood through a functional cycle (sometimes translated as 'circle') – the processes by which an organism perceives external stimuli and responds to them. He hypothesized a series of interconnected worlds: the *world-as-sensed* (or 'sum of stimuli'), the *inner world* (as created for itself by the animal), the *world-of-action* (external actions by the animal), and the *surrounding-world* or *Umwelt* (a combination of the *world of action* and the *world as sensed*).[40] *Umwelt*, then, is the world particular to the animal that is the product of receiving sensory information and acting upon it. As individual organisms, we do not have an identical *Umwelt* to anyone else. However, shared biological capacities and locations in the world mean that there are significant overlaps between individuals of the same and even of different species.[41]

Uexküll's *Umwelt* can be deduced from entirely biological processes: most significantly the 'functional cycle' of perceptual inputs and responses between the organism and its environment. I inhabit much the same physical space as my dog Benny, but we each have our distinctive *Umwelt* because the meaning of objects in the environment is different for each of us. Our sensory receptors and brain processing capacities are quite different,

36 Uexküll 1935/2010, 43; see Canguilhem 1965/2008.
37 Uexküll 1926, 16; cf Kant 1781/1929, 152–155 (B132–136).
38 Uexküll 1926, 40.
39 Ibid.
40 Ibid, 126–127.
41 Ferreira and Caldas 2013.

our responses vary considerably, as do how we relate to things (the toy, the couch, the book, the television, the ant, the raw meat) and whether we relate to them at all (a range of smells and sounds that I can't sense and the 'spoons, forks, matches. . . [that] do not exist for the dog because they are not meaning carriers'[42]). Hence our *Umwelts* – the lifeworlds we make by giving meaning to objects – are also quite distinct. Not only the mammals of the household, but also the passing (and sometimes inhabiting) birds and lizards, and the trillions of microbes, all have their distinctive *Umwelt*. Uexküll argued that the plants do not have *Umwelt* because they lack the organs needed to receive stimuli and enact effects, but they do nonetheless engage: 'The habitat of the plant, which is limited to the area around its location, transforms itself, from the plant's point of view, into a dwelling-integument consisting of various meaning-factors that are subject to regular change'.[43] By contrast, the rock, the fence post, the plastic rubbish bin, and the clouds moving in the wind, have no meaning-making capacities: 'the various shapes of the clouds are a product of the wind, and obey the law of cause and effect'.[44]

Ontological distinctions between plant and animal and between life and nonlife are, however, increasingly difficult to maintain. Over the past twenty-five years, plant ecologists and biologists have demonstrated that plants communicate, remember, learn, perceive, and create effects in their habitat.[45] Summarizing some of her studies with garden pea seedlings, Monica Gagliano says: 'By revealing that plants, too, are capable of associative learning and, consequently, qualified as proper subjects of cognitive research . . . these findings invite us to earnestly think about the vegetal mind'.[46] She 'insinuates' not only a 'what' but also a 'who' of plants – that is, subjectivity and emotion: 'plants too must evaluate their world *subjectively* and use their own experiences and feelings as functional states that motivate their choices'.[47] Plants do not necessarily think as humans do, as they do not have neurons, but they do nonetheless have a subjective ability to act (and, to return to Canguilhem, to create norms for their life) according to their own values – in particular, the value of continuing.

---

42 Uexküll 1982, 29.

43 Ibid, 36.

44 Ibid. Following the work of Prigogine and others studying complex systems, the attribution of 'the law of cause and effect' to cloud movement seems overly deterministic. At best, complex systemic factors produce such effects. But it is nonetheless correct to say that they do not make their own meanings.

45 Simard 2018; Gagliano 2018a.

46 Gagliano 2018a, 217; see also Gagliano 2018b; cf Turner and Somerville 2020.

47 Ibid, 218.

The notion of an internal experience of subjectivity is not a necessary or invariable component of emergent normativity: as I have indicated in Chapter 1 and will outline further in the next chapter, matter can follow a pathway, relate, act purposefully, and ultimately form patterns and systems without any internal experience or life. Nonetheless, the subjective experience of living matter is not inconsequential to certain forms of normativity, in particular the onto-epistemological engagements – perception, cognition, emotion – that rely on the self-felt *value* of life and the desire of living beings to persist, thrive, and replicate. Meaning, signification, and communication are constituted from these subjective engagements, resulting in distinctive characteristics and capacities for living things. The subjective existence of life is connected to the plural semiotic worlds of living collectives of organisms, both plants and animals. It gives rise to a second-order normativity associated with meanings and values – the information sharing between individuals in social groups and ultimately the prescriptions and directions, the institutions and bureaucracies, that subsist between living things.

Being and Co-becoming

The example of our household dog Benny is instructive in many ways. It is true that he possesses his own *Umwelt* that is quite different from that of other household members and that, as an independent organism, he creates norms for his own life that are partly derived from the norms he has acquired via evolution and co-evolution with humans over millennia. But – like all domestic animals and in particular companion animals[48] – his life and the human lives around him are shaped by a process of normative co-becoming, that is, by norms that we co-create. It is true that on my part (and on the part of my partner) the norms have been learnt abstractly from training manuals and classes that in turn reflect certain training and socialization narratives.[49] These abstract norms are then translated into daily routines and rules. But there are also a myriad of nuances, of capacities (ours and his), and the quirks of living together that particularize such forms.[50] Most importantly, of course, they have to be constantly brought into being by co-habiting – by the common performances, symbiotic and habitual, that embed the norm

---

48 See generally Haraway 2003; Gibson 2019.
49 Gibson 2019, 81–82; Haraway 2003, 40–47.
50 For instance, and to take only one of many possible dilemmas, the agency of the dog is highly constrained, and it is we, on the whole, who determine his life. As feminists, how then do we respond to what we read, possibly ineptly, as minor forms of resistance?

for us both so that when I tell him to 'sit' he generally does so and when I call his name there is some likelihood that he will come to me. There is no simple 'laying down the law' but rather a normative co-production.[51] In essentially the same way, training a rose vine (for instance) involves creating norms with the vine – working with its 'preferences' and plasticity of form to produce a particular shape.

Canguilhem's work on vital normativity represents a mid-twentieth-century perspective on the ways in which organisms not only live by but also create norms in order to maximize their own survival. As I indicated, despite some gestures towards ecology and environmental responsiveness and some expansive later additions to the main text of *The Normal and the Pathological*, Canguilhem's view is primarily organism-centric: it emphasizes the compulsion of the single entity rather than its relational existence and its co-productive capacities and reliances. Canguilhem's work is significant for the analysis of emergent normativity that it contains and its solid location of norm creation in convergence and difference in life forms and across zones of social life. However, the analysis of normative complexity and the intersections and interruptions that constitute eco-normativity can be taken further. Similarly, Jakob von Uexküll's analysis of *Umwelt* as the subjective bubble of being/meaning produced between an organism and its immediate exterior is centred – as all perception must be – on local and immediate relationships. But questions remain about how this individual perceptive world becomes shared and how the collective and cross-species relations that are constitutive of entities are normative.

It would take more space than I have available in this short book to explore fully these normative co-becomings. However, it seems obvious that the entirety of living matter is replete with normative engagements. This can be seen by putting together the vital normativity of theorists such as Canguilhem with what is increasingly known from a scientific perspective (and which has been known for much longer by Indigenous peoples) about ecosystems and complex emergent systems. Twenty-first-century bio-theory has moved decisively towards the understanding that biological processes take the form of multiple layers and feedback loops from which organisms emerge and co-emerge. This complex of relationships includes most importantly the connections and intra-actions between organisms facilitated by the porosity of their boundaries even as they maintain some kind of conditional autonomy. Relations between organisms of the same

---

51 And frequent misinterpretations on both sides. Does his bark signify 'danger!', 'help!' or 'give it to me!'? See Haraway 2003, 45.

species and cross-species connections are part of a broader pattern of the co-emergence of organism and habitat. Evolutionary narratives are no longer confined to the struggle of individuals to adapt to a changing environment or to compete with others for resources. Rather, organisms change their environment as well as change in response to it – they co-become with other organisms and with their *Umwelt*. It is interesting to observe at this point that habit, habitus, habitat, inhabit, habitation, and habituate connect a range of ideas concerning regularized connection to self, place, and others: having, being, dwelling, place, and the cognition involved in habituation.[52]

These generative processes occur at massive evolutionary scales that change the Earth's geology and chemistry,[53] and I will consider some of the implications of this in the next chapter. Co-becoming also typically occurs between life forms at local scales of shorter but nonetheless evolutionary duration, such as the symbiotic relationships that have formed between ants and butterflies.[54] In evolutionary history, the becoming-together of simple cells to form complex cells allowing, in time, the evolution of macro-organisms like slugs and human beings is possibly the ultimate in co-becoming: the process of endosymbiosis, confirmed experimentally by Lynn Margulis, consists of a relation between two simple bits of life (archaea and bacteria) producing cells with a nucleus, the foundation for complex living things like humans.[55] Moreover, according to Margulis, symbiosis is the main driver of evolutionary change – not just in deep time, but in an ongoing sense.[56] The process has been described evocatively (in this instance, at several removes[57]) by Donna Haraway: 'Critters interpenetrate one another, loop around and through one another, eat each other, get indigestion, and partially digest and partially assimilate one another, and thereby establish sympoietic arrangements that are otherwise known as cells, organisms, and ecological assemblages'.[58] In this way, Haraway generalizes symbiogenesis

---

52 See the discussion of slime mould habituation in Chapter 1.
53 See eg Eichenseer et al 2019; Wilcox 2019.
54 Gilbert et al 2012, 328; Fiedler et al 1996.
55 Margulis 2010; Sagan and Margulis 2013.
56 In evolutionary theory the failure of neo-Darwinism or the 'modern synthesis' (of Darwin and Mendel) – an emphasis on genetic essentialism and adaptation by mutation – is frequently mentioned in the literature. The technical details are sadly beyond my expertise but the image that emerges is that symbiotic life forms are foundational to evolution. Change via mutation within organisms occurs but is not the sole or even the primary driving force of evolution. See Margulis 2010; Sagan and Margulis 2013.
57 Haraway is in fact describing a painting by Shoshanah Dubiner that interprets Lynn Margulis' research on symbiogenesis.
58 Haraway 2016, 58.

as described by Margulis to 'sympoiesis' so that materials other than bio-logical entities can be included in the understanding of becoming-together: sympoiesis, she says, means 'making with' and is a 'word for worlding with, in company'.[59] All creation is co-creation (and, at the macro level, it is hard to know what the alternative would look like despite the European obsession with individual creativity). The unified and separate organism is not the archetype of life or the engine of evolution. Rather organisms are symbiotic assemblages: composed of multiple symbionts, becoming with others, symbiogenetically emergent, and only derivatively individual.

Whereas autopoiesis emphasizes self-creation, system, and operational closure, 'sympoiesis' names the interconnection and co-emergence, becoming together, of organisms and of organisms and habitat. Considered expansively, it includes all of the matter and meanings that are used to 'make together'. In biology, autopoiesis and symbiosis co-exist – they describe different but related processes and therefore do not contradict each other, despite their different emphases on autonomy and co-emergence. But symbiogenesis precedes autopoiesis and always accompanies it – autonomy is only possible because of relation and co-creation. As Cahoone put it: 'auto-control, auto-*nomos*, auto-*poiesis* do correctly identify one core distinctiveness of live organisms, as long as we understand they are only achievable through interaction with, and past selection by, the environment'.[60] Flow and co-becoming always precede distinct emergent forms, always co-exist with autonomous form, and always endure beyond them.

Both autopoiesis and – more recently – sympoiesis have been used to explore legal systems and legality. I will come back to these applications in more detail in Chapter 5, but briefly, autopoiesis is a biological *analogy* for legal systems and sympoiesis is both analogical and literal. Autopoiesis has been extensively deployed to account for law's apparent autonomy and its closed-open structure.[61] By contrast, in the evocative work of Anna Grear, 'sympoietic normativity' involves connection between the material interchanges of living systems and human norm-creating activities.[62] Within an ecological framing in which human social meanings co-exist with, flow into and out of, and emerge together with the biological, the geological, the animal, the microbial, the collective, and the individual, it becomes impossible to locate norms within only one zone of existence.

59 Ibid, 58. The term was coined by M Beth Dempster and has been extensively elaborated upon by Donna Haraway.

60 Cahoone 2013, 177.

61 Eg Luhmann 1992; Teubner 1992.

62 Grear 2020. See also Petersmann 2021.

Conclusion

Living norms exist in the imperative of organisms to survive and avoid pain, to grow, and to replicate. They are the product of life's ongoing experimentalism; following pathways that work and re-forming incrementally as needed. Living norms also emerge from the space in between existent entities living in an environment, creating and shaping habitat. In the process of living, norms emerge from engagement with the physical world exterior to the organism and its subjective production of an *Umwelt* distinctive to itself. The extent to which nonliving nature can also be said to be normative will be considered in the next chapter.

4   Geolaw as Flow and Stasis

Introduction

So far, I have presented normativity as aligned with teleology or purpose-driven action, accepting the dictum that where there is teleology in action there is also a norm.[1] I have emphasized two 'mechanisms' or material processes of normative becoming; these essentially frame the ways in which teleologies move forward or follow a direction. The first of these is centred on the notion of convergence and/or repetition, and includes habits and customs, pathways and performances, that stabilize modes of being and becoming as 'normal' and normative. Repetition includes of course the possibility of divergence and therefore of intentional, accidental, or emergent change – its modality is high probability not necessity. Repetition is always iteration.[2] The second 'mechanism' associated with normative becoming is connection, contract, or co-becoming, and is associated with the symbiotic processes out of which life is formed and evolves at the micro-scale and continues at the macro-scale. Although I have distinguished habit-repetition and connection-contract as separate processes, they are always co-implicated. A symbiotic relationship does not occur just once, but only produces a norm when it is repeated and habitual; a contract between human beings may appear to be a single event but is only possible because of longstanding socio-legal conventions and practices that precede it. Establishing a pathway through repetition may be a more intrinsic self-contained process, but one which nonetheless involves at every point both the differentiation of the same repeated action from other possible actions *and* the potentiality of divergence to a different pathway. The other is always present in the same.

---

1 Okrent 2017; Barham 2012.
2 Derrida 1988, 53.

DOI: 10.4324/9781003128335-5

To what extent can the image of normativity as iterative, connective, and teleological be seen in nonliving nature? From one perspective, it might seem implausible even to consider the question. Legal theory in the western tradition generally understands normativity and especially law as necessarily associated with acts of will, commands, or at least deliberate action. Social norms that have developed via habits and customs are subject to reflective identification and judgement – even where patterns of behaviour have developed without the deliberate intervention of any person or group, such norms can always be noticed, considered, and contested, even if they remain at least equally resistant to change compared with mere legislated norms. However, the account of normality and normativity that I have advanced does not rely on intention or deliberation or indeed self-aware behaviour. At no point do these dimensions of normativity require anything more than agency, understood in the minimal (and possibly tautologous) sense of an ability of an entity, system, or group to act or react. Subjectivity or selfhood is not necessary. Most pertinently, there is no need to show the presence of a subject who can decide, intend, or even desire or want. As I argued in Chapter 3, the presence of subjects produces plural and shared normative worlds invested with value and communicable meanings. But normativity can emerge without meaning-producing subjects.

However, the attribution of normativity (as opposed to mechanical-physical laws) to nonliving things is not necessarily straightforward. Nonliving things clearly act; they are agents, and exert a power and a force on other things.[3] But how are these actions normative? In what sense can the forceful actions of nonliving matter acting in the absence of life (the flow of water, the dissipation of energy, the bonding and decay of atoms, etc) be said to be driven by purposes? In what sense are the predictable pathways of matter formed by iterations and connections that are directed and probable (ie norm creating) rather than merely mechanical? These are questions that I clearly can't answer myself but, as with philosophical biology, there is much written on such topics that extends towards legal and political thought, and that might be brought into the field of legal theory.[4] Beyond these conversations within the domain of physics and chemistry, there is of course the continuity between the living and the nonliving that needs to be considered theoretically. In this chapter I start by considering the philosophical resonance of the western hegemonic separation of living from nonliving things. I then look at the continuities and flows between life

---

3 Barad 2007, 2010. See also generally De Landa 2000.
4 The work of Karen Barad on matter and mattering is fundamental here. I will come to it later in the chapter.

and nonlife that characterize the dynamics of planet Earth, with a focus on water and energy flow as encapsulating the sameness and difference, order and novelty, characteristic of all emergent normativity.

Life and Nonlife

Before looking at the normativity of nonliving matter, it is helpful to think about the differences between life and nonlife that have activated philosophical interest. Is there a clear distinction to be drawn between life and nonlife? In even posing this question I am situating myself within a very particular epistemological framework: one in which life and nonlife are divisible and identifiable, perhaps by modes of categorization and theorization, combined with empirical observations. This is a question underpinned by a pervasive 'biochauvinism' or assumption that life is special.[5] Putting aside marginal cases of categorization (such as viruses), distinctions are commonly made that separate the living from the dead and from the never alive. In western theory,[6] these distinctions tend to honour, and accord moral status to, the living over the nonliving. However, even in law, it is increasingly recognized that some complex systems challenge this extant divisibility between living and nonliving: in legislating for river recognition, the Aotearoa New Zealand Parliament has declared 'Te Awa Tupua is an indivisible and living whole from the mountains to the sea, incorporating the Whanganui River and all of its physical and metaphysical elements'.[7] When speaking of an entire river system as an entity accorded legal subjecthood, it is impossible to distinguish its living from its nonliving constituents. The fish, the plants that sustain them, the riverbed, the tributaries, and the water become part of a single living system.

Within the lifeworld created by a western secular perspective, the distinction between life and nonlife seems to be such a common-sense part of everyday life that it is not really necessary to subject it to scrutiny. But the fact that this distinction is not culturally universal and the fact that daily life (such as the circulation of matter and the existence of the living river system) constantly puts it into question means that it is worth taking a closer look at its theoretical dimensions. There are many ways of differentiating life from nonlife. Many science-based definitions of life focus on biological processes: the fact that living beings replicate, evolve, metabolize, maintain homeostasis and their own boundaries, grow, die, and so forth. Such

---

5 Wolfe 2014, 2015 (on Canguilhem).
6 There have been many notable critics of the division, such as AN Whitehead (1938).
7 *Te Awa Tupua (Whanganui River Claims Settlement) Act 2017* (NZ) s 12.

processes are irreversible and temporal; they control entropy (that is, they actively control energy flow and prevent the onset of the decay that takes over with death). The forms produced by the processes of life are highly constrained: newly evolved forms build upon past forms. But they are not determined. Living form is characterized by its plasticity,[8] for instance by the combination of nature and nurture that produces a body, by the fact that I will change shape if I exercise more or less, that my brain makes new pathways as I learn things, that species adapt to altered environments, but also shape them. In countering the mechanical view of life, Daniel Nicholson notes that machines are either on or off, whereas life is always on, even if dormant; machines are reactive, whereas life is active.[9] Machines are the sum of their parts, while organisms and collectivities are far more than the sum of their parts. Machines are designed, whereas organisms are self-organizing.[10] Such objective and observable characteristics may supply clusters of criteria that can be used to describe living things and to differentiate them broadly from the nonliving (which do not reproduce, evolve, etc) but the attempt to draw a bright-line distinction via a single definition of life has proved futile for science. Life is too diverse, there are always borderline cases (such as the virus), and any set of criteria ends up including some but not other 'living' entities.[11] Unsurprisingly, some definitions – in the attempt to reduce life to a unified description – end up including things that, at least to a western mind, are clearly not alive.[12] Moreover, the definitional contestations that take place within science say little about what it is to *be* alive as an experience.

Up to the beginning of the twentieth century, ideas describing the distinctive qualities of life, while avoiding completely disembodied forces such as a soul, were captured in an array of philosophical notions that imagined life as encapsulating some defining characteristic – for instance, *conatus*, *elan vital*, *Bildungstrieb*, and entelechy.[13] The early twentieth-century biophilosophers surveyed in Chapter 3 focused on understanding life from the inside, rather than critiquing the boundary between life and nonlife. It is therefore

---

8 See eg Plessner 1928/2019, 116.

9 Nicholson 2018, 153.

10 Kant 1790/1952; Fox Keller 2007a.

11 See Cleland 2019; Machery 2012.

12 The computer virus is sometimes mentioned in this context, as are computer simulations, flames, and crystals. See Cleland 2019, 36–45.

13 *Conatus* (the desire to continue) is usually associated with Spinoza; *elan vital* with Bergson; entelechy (actualization of potential) with Aristotle and Driesch; *Bildungstrieb* (formative drive) with Blumenbach and Kant. See generally Bennett 2010, 62–81.

unsurprising that there is a tendency within such works for the distinction to be reinforced – in some cases this is inevitable. Canguilhem's description of vital normativity does not seem suited to nonlife; indeed, in his work there is a clear difference between life and nonlife: life is characterized by the existence of self-created normativity associated with a kind of subjectivity. As Anne Marie Mol put it, 'Canguilhem warned that there is a qualitative difference between the physical and chemical laws that govern particles and the norms that mark the difference between viable biological order and the chaos that comes with death'.[14] The organism, unlike the rock, *itself* makes, follows, and re-makes the norms it needs to survive and to avoid suffering. Life forms *want* to continue, to grow, and to multiply. Although already formed by multiple biological layers formed across an evolutionary scale, the norm-following and creating dimension of the organism has an ongoing and active not just reactive quality.

As I outlined in Chapter 3, other early twentieth-century biophilosophers also described life in terms that implicitly or explicitly distinguished it from nonlife, albeit using different theoretical languages. Jakob von Uexküll theorized a subjective perceptive bubble around each organism. Organisms receive stimuli according to their own capabilities and those of their species and act within a confined zone of influence, thus forming an *Umwelt*. Organisms also have an *Innenwelt* or entirely subjective world, which is missing from nonliving entities. Helmuth Plessner argued that organisms have both boundary and positionality.[15] From the outside, the organism's boundary locates it in physical space. From the point of view of the organism itself, that is, from the inside, the boundary provides the organism with the bodily limit of its unfolding life and thus an experience of its self. 'This does not mean', Plessner said, 'that a thing that appears as alive is completely different from things in general'.[16] Plessner also pointed out,

> A frog or a palm tree is subject to the same phenomenal laws of thinghood (not to mention the broad zone of continuous physical commonalities) as is a stone or a shoe. It is only that animate things in relation to inanimate ones have the surplus of that mysterious property of life, which, despite its nature as a property, materially changes not only the appearance of the particular thing, but also formally its *mode* of appearance.[17]

---

14 Mol 1998, 275. See also Wolfe 2014, 2015.
15 Plessner 1928/2019.
16 Ibid, 84.
17 Ibid.

Thus, a shoe or a stone has a boundary that places its form in space, but only a *life* form has a boundary which is part of its identity and self-experience.

Such differentiations of life from nonlife have also at times provided the basis for categorizations within life. Working with a model of plants that now seems outdated, Uexküll distinguished between plants and animals on the basis that a plant does not have a nervous system, perceptual organs, or the means of effecting change outside itself.[18] Plessner's project in philosophical anthropology fundamentally concerned *levels* of organic life, in which humans were described distinctively as having a reflective capacity not shared by nonhuman animals. That this appears evident from the human point of view does not invalidate the possibility that nonhuman beings have other capacities that might be equally valuable. Nor do we have any independent nonhuman standard according to which an assessment of *levels* can be made.

How do distinctions between life and nonlife and between forms of life affect an analysis of norms and normativity?[19] From a conventional human and Euro-colonial perspective, such distinctions matter a great deal. Taking humans, our ability to deliberate collectively and individually and, through such deliberation, create complex systems of norms means that we see ourselves as having norm-creating powers that other parts of nature do not – as far as we know – possess. We can devise planning and environmental legal systems to manage the destruction and protection of nonhuman worlds. We can regard ourselves as intentionally co-constructing norms with nonhuman life[20] – such as when we train a dog or a rose bush. We hubristically regard the co-production as directed on the human side, even though it is only possible through the distinctive agency and life form of the rose bush or the dog. Microbial life is far more influential than we are: not only do microbes respond agentially to their environment as individuals; collectively they engineer habitat for all life forms with processes such as those that result in the production of atmospheric gases or of biomass. Such normative creation and co-creation are more difficult to perceive in relation to nonlife because the creative agential aspect appears to be entirely on the side of the human. But is this correct? Do the nonliving play no part? Humans can only make plastic from fossilized life because of the intrinsic chemical properties of the extracted material. Our pathways and roads are in part determined by the contours and other characteristics of the land.

---

18 Uexküll 1982, 33.
19 See generally Aston and Davies 2022.
20 An instance of Grear's (2020) 'sympoietic normativity'. See Chapter 5, below.

The sculptor responds to the properties of the stone and does not merely force a mental shape onto it. More importantly and fundamentally, life has, at some point, emerged from nonlife. Therefore, despite the more obvious family resemblances between the factors that produce living and human normativity (subjectivity, desire to continue), it seems implausible that the story of norm creation stops with life.

Material Flows: Water and Energy

Material continuity between the living and the nonliving is evident from fact that nonliving materials are constantly cycling through living systems. Plants are exemplary in this sense, because they make their own food from materials that have never been alive.[21] Using the energy of sunlight and with the assistance of soil microbes, plants combine carbon dioxide and water to make glucose. They draw nutrients such as nitrogen and potassium from the soil. For this reason, plants do not need to be as mobile as animals, but they can nonetheless communicate across long distances via underground networks of mycorrhizal fungi.[22] For animals, the circulation of nonliving (and never-alive) materials occurs via our ability (or the ability of our microbiomes) to convert oxygen into carbon dioxide and the ubiquitous biochemical use of water in a large number of metabolic reactions.[23] Animals are incapable of making our own food from materials that have never been alive. Our nutrition must, at some point, have been captured and pre-processed by plants.

The circulation of nonliving matter through life provides a starting point for thinking about the boundary between life and nonlife. It engenders a perception that, across the plane of metabolic flows, there is in fact no such clear distinction. Moreover, it may appear that these exchanges of matter are driven by life and in particular by microbes, which occupy and control the life-nonlife boundary.[24] Hence it is life that produces glucose, converts matter into energy and so forth. The agency of all life forms in interacting with and shaping their habitat is also well established. But it is not necessarily the case that agency lies only on the side of the living. From another perspective, it can be argued that life is equally engineered by nonlife – for instance that life is a consequence of the fact that energy from the sun dissipates or that the forms of life that exist are produced by the agency

---

21 Plants are 'autotrophs'; animals are 'heterotrophs'.
22 Simard 2018; Simard et al 2012.
23 Frenkel-Pinter et al 2021.
24 Margulis and Sagan 1995 (drawing on Whitehead); Clark and Hird 2013.

of water.[25] Indeed, to ask whether life or nonlife is the prime driver of the complex systems that we exist within suggests a foundational and linear thinking that fails to accommodate the cycling, recycling, feedback loops, and indeterminacies of complex systems.

Water and energy flow have often been used both metaphorically and literally by theorists wanting to capture the movement of matter and the temporary stability of life and other material forms within this constant flow. 'Flow' in these discussions is never just an uninterrupted stream: it is the resistance, deviation, and perturbations interrupting the stream which produce order. For instance, as mentioned in Chapter 2, in 1799 Friedrich Schelling described 'every original product of Nature', including organisms, as whirlpools formed by 'resistance' in a stream, in 1817 Georges Cuvier said that 'life is a vortex, more or less rapid, more or less complicated', and in 2000 Carl Woese described organisms as 'resilient patterns in a turbulent flow'.[26] In counterposing a prevailing 'mechanical concept of the organism' with a 'stream of life concept', Daniel Nicholson concludes that, '[w]hatever else organisms may be, what cannot be denied is that they are stable metabolic flows of energy and matter'.[27] In such a description, it is the *flow* of a nonliving substance that precedes, enables, and regulates the living.

Ancient atomism, in particular as expounded by Lucretius,[28] is a precursor of all of these images of turbulent flow. Lucretius described the *clinamen*: the imperceptible and indeterminate deviation or *swerve* in an otherwise parallel (ie 'laminar') flow that engenders collisions between atoms, leading to turbulence, and eventually to the entirety of the natural world.[29] Without the swerve 'no collisions between primary elements would occur, and no blows would be effected, with the result that nature would never have created anything'.[30] The unpredictable – probabilistic – occurrence of the swerve is, according to Lucretius, the source of free

---

25 Frenkel-Pinter et al 2021; Schneider and Kay 1994; Schneider and Sagan 2005, 38.

26 Schelling 1799/2004, 18; Cuvier, quoted in Nicholson 2018, 149; Woese 2004, 176. See generally Nicholson 2018.

27 Nicholson 2018, 162.

28 Lucretius wrote *De Rerum Natura* (On the Nature of Things) as an exposition of Epicurean atomism, though the most famous part, the 'atomic swerve' is 'not mentioned in any extant work of Epicurus . . . though it is possible that it was referred to in a passage now lost': Bailey 1947, 839. *De Rerum Natura* was written in the first century BC – its emphasis on the 'free will' of matter stands in contrast to the determinism of Democritus.

29 Lucretius, *De Rerum Natura* II, lines 217–293 (see eg translation by Smith: Lucretius 2001, 40–42); see summary by Prigogine and Stengers 1984, 141; cf Bailey 1947, 838–842.

30 Lucretius 2001, 41.

will.[31] Lucretius' ideas have been rehabilitated by Michel Serres, and cited approvingly by Ilya Prigogine and Isabelle Stengers.[32] Serres notes the paradox of turbulence: that it appears to introduce disorder into a steady flow, but in fact it becomes the origin of order:

> The physical theory of turbulence creates a paradox. Laminar flow, the figure of chaos, is at first sight a model of order. The atoms pour out in parallel, without mixing or sticking to each other. . . . Turbulence seems to introduce a disorder into this arrangement. This is what the language means: *turbare* means a disorder, a confusion, a disruption or, as we say, a perturbation. Disorder emerges from order.
> Yet it is precisely the reverse that is to be described and that occurs. Physics tries to explain how things and the world are formed naturally out of the atomic chaos, in other words how an order, or several orders, emerge from disorder. And it is turbulence that secures the transition.[33]

Serres counterposes two forms of chaos from Lucretius: random atomic chaos and the chaos of parallel flow. But the vortex arising from turbulence is set against both as the emergence of complex order from simple chaos: 'The vortex is unstable and stable, fluctuating and in equilibrium, is order and disorder at once'.[34] Though the details may differ, there is much that is prescient of complexity theory in the account offered by Lucretius.[35] After all, one vortex eventually dissipates but the reality is plural: 'The world is a vortex of vortices, interlacings or networks of waves'.[36] Most importantly for my purposes, 'flow' is normatively suggestive – a flow is neither the chaotic movement of particles in a state of equilibrium nor the parallel streams of untouching particles. Flow is directional sameness with built-in divergence and connection. As the anterior of order, is the turbulent flow of matter and energy also pre-normative? Is flow the *persistent but resisted* movement from which norms and normality arise?

Both water and energy seem to speak to the relationship between order and chaos implied by flow. They are both with and without form. Water and energy are going somewhere: they move in a directional fashion and hence are teleological and temporal. As ancient elements, fire and water subsist

31 Ibid.
32 Serres 1977/2000; Prigogine and Stengers 1984, 141.
33 Serres 1977/2000, 27.
34 Ibid, 30.
35 See Webb 2000.
36 Serres 1977/2000, 50.

between the (apparent) solidity of earth and the ethereal quality of air. Water and energy are structured and directed in their flow, somewhat stable as presences, but endlessly dynamic and full of multiple potentials. They are not alone in these properties (air and rock also flow) but they provide a good starting place for illustrating the normative qualities that emerge from flowing materials. At some level, water and energy are therefore emblematic of a normativity that emerges in the interplay of sameness and difference and, ultimately, necessity and chance.

Water

Given the constant, basic, and ubiquitous influence of water, it should perhaps not be surprising that rivers feature so prominently in current efforts to attribute legal status and/or rights to natural objects.[37] Giving human beings access to water is clearly necessary to our continued existence and allowing all of life to have access to water is equally imperative. Water is primary – everything and everyone relies on it. Sometimes, the normative import of river systems is framed as a 'right to life' of the river.[38] At other times, it is framed as a statement of obligation on humans to look after the river. For example, in 2017, the state legislature of Victoria, Australia, passed an Act to protect the Birrarung (Yarra River). In the voice of the local custodians of the river, the Woi-rurung, the preamble to the Act states that '[t]he Birrarung is alive, has a heart, a spirit, and is part of our Dreaming'.[39] The statement goes on to assert the Woi-rurung obligation to 'keep the Birrarung alive', an obligation that the Act extends to public entities making certain decisions that affect the river. Such statements and legislative enforcements are significant: framed in the institutions of the colonizers, they acknowledge and bring a limited recognition of the intrinsic normative – norm-creating – qualities of human-river relationships. But they do not, in themselves, channel this normativity because they utilize a structure – a separate human institution – constructed from (and for) human exceptionalism. The image presented by such statements is nonetheless one of engagement in a normative pluriverse whereby the legislative action intersects with an agential river system replete with meanings and norms.

---

37 O'Donnell 2019; Clark et al 2019.
38 See eg the Fitzroy River Declaration, discussed in RiverOfLife et al 2020. See also Clark et al 2019.
39 *Yarra River Protection (Wilip-gin Birrarung murron) Act 2017* (Vic) preamble. *Wilip-gin Birrarung murron* means 'Keep the Birrarung alive'. See also O'Donnell 2019 and, relating to Cape York Peninsula, Langton 2006.

Elizabeth Povinelli relates a story originating thousands of kilometres away from Birrarung, from the Indigenous people of Northern Australia. The story concerns a creek-teenager, Tjipel, who forms a boundary between two language groups and connects these groups to other areas.[40] Dressed in male clothes and carrying a spear, Tjipel travelled along the coast. After a fight with an old man, Tjipel became a creek. However, her temporal existence does not follow the western linearity of 'which came first, second, or third',[41] and nor is she a single body of water with objective characteristics. She is only known through interaction, has 'multiple forms and versions', within which are 'multiple modes, qualities, and relations'.[42] One of the many notable features of Tjipel as described by Povinelli concerns the mutual normative expectations that arise between her and any humans who relate in any way to her. Povinelli describes what Ruby Yilngi, her research collaborator, told her:

> Tjipel and her kin were internal to each other's arrangement. Tjipel established an estuarine normativity that sought to compel humans to care about and for her – minding her legs by hunting in her mangroves, walking along her spear thrower, fishing in her creek, et cetera. If Yilngi's family acceded to the watery norms Tjipel established, Tjipel would turn toward Yilngi's family and care for them. If this rapport was broken, Tjipel would not die, but she would turn away from her human kin.[43]

The mutual normative obligations held by Tjipel and those who live in her vicinity are based on care and continuing co-existence. In the way Povinelli describes these norms, they emerge in densely interconnected places, beings, and actions. They are intrinsic to all life. In the terms I have been using in this book, the norms are embedded both in the characteristics of the water itself – that it has flow and purpose – and the connections or obligative bonds between the water and its co-dependents.

Within the western world view, however, the normative qualities and relations intrinsic to water seem more difficult to perceive, despite the necessity of water to all life. That water is essential is never in doubt, but – despite the agency associated with (for instance) holy water – it is frequently seen as merely a medium, cleaning fluid, solvent, or lubricant rather than as an

---

40 This is an extremely truncated summary of Povinelli's narrative, itself a concise re-telling from conversations over many years with the Indigenous people of the locality. See Povinelli 2016, 92ff.
41 Ibid, 93.
42 Ibid, 94.
43 Ibid.

active participant in ecosocial relations. Against these common associations, Astrida Neimanis says:

> We are created in water, we gestate in water, we are born into an atmosphere of diffuse water, we drink water, we harbour it, it sustains and protects us, it leaves us – we are always, to some extent, in it. The passage from body of water to body of water is never merely metaphoric but radically material.[44]

Water is pervasive and has been shown to be the central participant in biochemical reactions. Our constant need for water is explained by the fact that life consists primarily of chemical reactions involving water. Frenkel-Pinter et al argue that '[w]ater is transformative and is transformed, eternally causing change and constantly changing. Water is the gate-keeper and the matrix'.[45] They suggest that water guided the emergence of life because it can react with (ie dissolve, transform, bond to) some but not other molecules: 'pre-biotic chemical selection, leading to life, was substantially directed by water'.[46] Water on its own did not produce life but, in a non-trivial sense, water *regulated* the emergence of life and it regulates the continuance of life. Water is there enabling and directing at every step of the way, not only in life but across all systems that engage in the hydrological cycle. Life also intervenes in and structures the flow of water: beavers, like humans, are hydraulic engineers. The emergence of hydrosocial studies (and its use of terms such as 'hydrosocial cycle' and 'hydrosocial territories') consciously attends to the human and nonhuman assemblages that constitute a 'waterscape'.[47] Waterscapes are human-nonhuman co-creations. Thus the normativity of waterscapes is multidimensional – it consists in human and nonhuman interventions in lakes, rivers, oceans, aquifers, etc, but also in the intrinsic regulative powers of water, and even in its directed and always potentially turbulent flow.

Energy

The study of thermodynamics also provides some fascinating, if at first sight unlikely, insights into the normativity of nonliving processes and their

---

44 Neimanis 2009, 164.
45 Frenkel-Pinter et al 2021, 7.
46 Ibid.
47 Linton and Budds 2014; Boelens et al 2016; Swyngedouw 1999; Karpouzoglou and Vij 2017.

connection to living systems, including human life and law.[48] Thermodynamics is the science of energy flow. As Eric Schneider and Dorion Sagan note, energy does not literally 'flow' because it is not a fluid but flowing is nonetheless an apt and helpful metaphor.[49] For instance, energy 'flows' out of a hot cup of coffee into the surrounding cool air. The second law of thermodynamics states,[50] essentially, that energy flow or dissipation has a *direction*. Energy does not move from cold to hot but rather the other way around. The hot coffee becomes cool because it loses energy to the air. After a lapse of time, the temperatures of the coffee and the air are equalized – they reach a state of 'equilibrium'. This exceedingly simple (and simplistic) example can be associated with a number of incredibly significant insights. The directedness of the flow of energy is associated with the 'arrow of time' or the fact that time appears to have a direction and always moves towards equilibrium or disorder.[51] This movement of time stands in contrast to Newton's mechanical universe, the equations for which are apparently reversible: physicists say that Newton's physical laws work equally well in reverse – the billiard balls *could* be moving in the opposite direction and the equations would work equally well. The apparent forward direction of time therefore seems problematic in Newton's universe, or at least unaccounted for by its fundamental mechanical laws. This is not the case for energy dissipation. Ilya Prigogine notes that both reversibility and irreversibility co-exist: 'Nature involves both *time-reversible* and *time-irreversible* processes, but it is fair to say that irreversible processes are the rule and reversible processes the exception'.[52]

Energy flow always has a direction in time and space: having lost its warmth to the cool air, the coffee does not, without further intervention, become hot – there is no going backwards. The orderly situation, whereby the coffee is hot and the air cool, becomes the more disorderly situation whereby the coffee is, at best, tepid. The entropy of the coffee-air system

---

48 As always, my comprehension of scientific matters is general and sketchy, but see Schrödinger 1944/1992; Prigogine 1997; Schneider and Sagan 2005; Rovelli 2018.

49 Sagan and Schneider 2005, 38; Schneider and Kay 1994.

50 The first law of thermodynamics concerns the conservation of energy: if a system is closed, the energy inside it is constant.

51 The idea of 'disorder' can be confusing – it means essentially a state where there is relatively less structure and is often illustrated by imagining a container divided into two parts, with a vacuum in one part and air in the other part. The distribution of the air is structured or orderly (ie through presence and absence). If a hole is opened between the two parts of the container, the molecules in the air will soon become evenly distributed, losing their structure and becoming more disorderly.

52 Prigogine 1997, 18.

has increased. If left for days, the coffee will evaporate, and then, after thousands of years or longer, the cup will also disintegrate – entropy or disorder increasing all the time. An increase in entropy is, in this example, an increase in disorder and, without some intervention that modifies the process, the direction is always towards increasing entropy. It may be overstating matters to say that energy *wants* to spread but it nonetheless has a teleological aspect – it does proceed *towards* something. Sagan and Margulis say that '[t]hermoregulation . . . appears not to be one teleological process among others, but a sort of originary, nonliving purposefulness'.[53]

Interestingly, however, energy dissipation does not only create disorder – it also creates structure.[54] Prigogine, awarded a Nobel Prize for his work on far-from-equilibrium dissipative structures,[55] says 'we have now learned that it is precisely through irreversible processes associated with the arrow of time that nature achieves its most delicate and complex structures'.[56] The simplistic examples of the cup of coffee or the divided box of gases that many of us would have learnt about at secondary school produce correspondingly simplified images of linear change: but everything is vastly more complex and almost nothing is actually isolated from multiple connections and interactions. Energy spreads, and in so doing it fluctuates, bifurcates, cycles back on itself, draws in energy from the environment, renews itself, and in the process forms stable patterns, structures, systems, and complexities.[57]

Energy and matter therefore become self-organizing and increasingly complex – for instance as weather patterns, stable and self-reproducing chemical formations, and ultimately as living beings in complex interconnected ecosystems. Considered from the perspective of thermodynamics, life is one dimension of the vast dynamics of energy flow, a process that is not random but directed and purposeful. The fact that organisms are able to stave off disintegration for a while does not mean that we are somehow outside or different from entropic processes. Rather, as mentioned in Chapter 1, several scientists have argued that life appears to be one way for the

---

53 Sagan and Margulis 2013, 213.
54 Prigogine 1997, 26.
55 These are structures that dissipate energy but in the process create structure. Sagan and Margulis 2013 provide the following examples of common physical phenomena: tornados, whirlpools, Jupiter's red spot, and dust devils. Many more examples exist, and a living organism is also a self-organizing structure that cycles energy.
56 Prigogine 1997, 26.
57 This list of processes is gleaned from Prigogine 1997; Schneider and Sagan 2005; Jantsch 1980. Some of them have very technical meanings and descriptions.

Earth to channel the energy flow that is associated with increasing entropy.[58] Energy dissipates, and life assists in this dissipation.[59] From this point of view, once again, we can see that it is not only life that regulates energy but energy that guides and regulates life.

The systems produced by energy flow obviously do not exist in isolation but interact with each other as intersecting systems or, to return to Serres' exposition of Lucretius, a 'vortex of vortices'.[60] That which began as a 'singular atomic cascade' becomes 'a multiplicity of rivers, streaming by all paths, transverse, diagonal, intersected, complex'.[61] But nor are such complex open systems reducible to physics – they describe intersecting formations that are not a unified totality, but a plurality of systems, that are social, ecological, and socio-ecological. There can be no unified or universal account of these intersecting systems, because they are based on unpredictable perturbations and interventions, they hybridize and adapt in non-standard ways, and they are constantly emergent – producing new forms that exceed the component parts that previously existed. At the scale of Earth systems, 'Gaia' brings all of these complex systems together in a non-unified, always dynamic, whole. State law is part of this socio-ecological plurality, even though for purposes of regulation, governance, management, and so forth, it imagines itself as outside.

Conclusion: Normative Flow

It seems to be the case, then, not only that life engineers lifeless matter, but also that the flow of energy and matter produces and guides life.[62] Life-nonlife engineering is bi-directional: much of the earth (limestone, peat, coal, etc) is made by life and vice versa. Most significantly, the apparently directed and purposive nature of the flow of energy and the regulating functions of water means that these agents, like organisms, are normative – perhaps not in exactly the same way that life is normative but nonetheless producing and following norms that are directed, irreversible, and based

---

58 Schneider and Sagan 2005 propose as a general principle that 'nature abhors a gradient' – in other words, that nature is constantly finding ways to flatten steep differences, for instance in air pressure, chemical concentrations, or temperature. The efforts that natural processes make to deal with such gradients serve as the basis for the emergence of life.

59 Schneider and Sagan 2005; Sagan and Margulis 2013; Lovelock and Margulis 1974.

60 Serres 1977/2000, 50.

61 Ibid.

62 Such a statement sounds deterministic, but the point is that the movement is probabilistic not determined; see Prigogine 1997.

on probabilities rather than the necessities of physical mechanisms.[63] The hydrosocial cycle, for instance, is not random but follows a vast and complex pattern constrained by intersecting geological, biological, atmospheric, and social (human and nonhuman) norms.

It is therefore certainly no longer far-fetched to claim that what western theorists commonly think of as the human *nomos* is in fact composed of not only nonhuman living normativities like those of our own microbiome, but also the normativities of nonliving nature (of which we are a product). As Ilya Prigogine put it, 'human creativity and innovation can be understood as the amplification of laws of nature already present in physics or chemistry'.[64] Or, as Sagan and Margulis put it: 'Our telic behaviours stem from those of nature'.[65] For these reasons, normative co-production is embedded across the life-nonlife boundary: in the making of living normativity there are constant crossings of this boundary and emergences from it. It is not possible to separate out the living part of nature as the site of normativity. That this is the case is not a recent invention of western knowledge. It appears, in fact, to have been ingrained in ancient cosmologies (as represented by Lucretius' rendition of Epicurean atomism), and supressed in the west for many hundreds of years. The idea that law is embedded in the land and waters that support all life has a much older, more developed, more secure, and enduring heritage in many First Nations knowledges.

63 Ibid.
64 Ibid, 71.
65 Sagan and Margulis 2013, 227.

5   Law, Nature, and Legal Theory

Introduction

These connections between bio-norms, eco-norms, geo-norms, and social norms that I have explored so far might seem a long way from the 'law' which is the ordinary material of legal theory. It may appear both too singular and too totalizing to read normativity across different ecological frames in this way, as well as a simplification and misrepresentation of more properly scientific descriptions. My aim is not (of course) to totalize, or for that matter to misrepresent, but rather to connect normativity across several registers. Thinking about the extended *nomos* in this way represents just one cut of many that are possible to add to other emerging efforts to connect the human and the nonhuman and to embed human law within an ecological materiality. In order to make connections, it is necessary to look for commonalities across spheres understood as different, an endeavour that necessitates simplification. However, the image I am attempting to construct is above all composed of multiplicities and fragments. Purposes, pathways, and connections might begin with singular actions or they might be embedded in fragmented evolutionary histories. But their interactions as norms are heterogeneous, coalescing and diverging in partial, conflicting, and inchoate situations.

Connectedness across spheres previously separated in anthropocentric thought has become a point of departure for contemporary theory: hence we have natureculture, socio-nature, biolegality, eco-society, bioculture, biogeology, cosmopolitics, and this book about ecolaw. To capture the connectedness of multiple things, Donna Haraway speaks of the creative scholarly process as compost.[1] When making compost 'it is well to remember that

---

1 Haraway 2016, 4.

DOI: 10.4324/9781003128335-6

in general, very large amounts of one kind of material only does not make good compost. The greater the variety of materials used at one time, the better will be the final product'.[2] (At the same time, if you are not careful you can end up with sludge.[3]) Taking the thought of connectivity across multiplicity as a starting point involves suspending theoretical certainties and boundaries. It involves suspending theory itself as a primarily conceptual project and trying to practise it as an embodied and material project. And indeed, it involves discarding the very idea of there being a starting point, either a beginning or an end, since nothing is static: everything is always in motion.

Socio-ecological co-becoming concerns the emergence of complex entities as bio-geo-socio-formations (where the 'socio-' also includes human law). The idea of *legal* co-becoming on a human plane is nothing new. Throughout the twentieth century, legal autonomy was often seen as a product of a process of normative co-becoming. Eugen Ehrlich's living law, Robert Cover's jurisgenesis in an expansive normative universe, and Patricia Ewick and Susan Silbey's work on legal consciousness are all variations on the theme of state law being produced out of quotidian legal practices and meanings in their interactions with broader socio-political normativities, environments, ideas, and patterns.[4] The knitting together of different normative systems into hybrids used for specific purposes has also been a feature of recent legal pluralism.[5] Until recently, the terminology of co-becoming and symbiosis was not associated with these insights, but it might nonetheless be used to describe their emphases on the emergence and change of state law in a context of social norms. What is missing from twentieth-century accounts of legal co-creation within human society is an account of the co-becomings of human *and nonhuman* normativities. Twentieth-century socio-legal theory, by and large (and with the exception of Indigenous knowledges), did not develop an explicit understanding that the nonhuman sphere is a site of normative emergence and that the human *nomos* connects with nonhuman jurisgenesis.

Within western theory, legal geography has been at the forefront of theorizing the co-becoming of human law with the nonhuman, understood by

---

2 Bennett 1989, 111. Or as Hamilton and Neimanis 2018, 502 say (building on Haraway building on Strathern), 'it matters what compostables make compost'. See also Turner and Somerville 2020.

3 I know this from experience.

4 Ehrlich 1962; Cover 1983; Ewick and Silbey 1998.

5 Griffiths 1998; von Benda-Beckmann and Turner 2018; cf Davies 2017a.

reference to the geographical category of place.[6] Recently, Robyn Bartel has used the theory of legal pluralism to describe the distinct normative systems of place and human law, which interact and hybridize. Legal geographers, she says, describe place as

> co-producing not just state and other laws, but its own legal order, comprising the unique biophysical and social features and constraints (ie 'rules') of place. These may interact and conflict with, as well as co-generate other legal orders, including scientific laws . . . Chemical and physical laws . . . control human behavior, as well as co-creating space and place. In turn, place law, co-created by us, is similarly controlling. It may restrict, permit and promote certain human behaviours, through the material, biophysical and social factors, and ecological geomorphological and cultural features of places. These may be localized but are not always bounded, or small in scale.[7]

Here, we get a glimpse of just how complex and analytically powerful legal plurality becomes when it is fully extended to biophysical registers. It is not only a question of human law co-becoming with the law of place, but of multiple orders understood as a confluence of norms intersecting, converging, and conflicting in specified situations. It is precisely along these lines that this book has developed, though with less emphasis on place as such, and more emphasis on the ongoing emergence of biological and geophysical norms. However, it must not be forgotten that these emergences are necessarily located. Legal geography has made huge inroads into shifting the conceptual resources of western legal theory in such a way as to enable law to be understood as materially connected, not only to the human societies that give it form but also to place and time, land, ecology, nonhuman life, and emergent intra-active realities.[8]

My purpose in this final substantive chapter is not to engage in detail with existing literature that connects human with nonhuman normativity, but rather to consider some key questions about how my depiction of a wider ecological *nomos* relates to adjacent concerns in legal theory, notably, 'how does it relate to natural law theory?', 'where does state-based positive law sit in this account?', and 'how can we understand the unity and

---

6 Blomley 2003, 2011; Delaney 2010; Blomley et al 2001; Braverman et al 2014; T O'Donnell et al 2020.
7 Bartel 2018, 65.
8 See eg Anker 2017.

distributed nature of legal *systems*, their closure and openness?'[9] I cannot fully answer these questions; the chapter provides only some preliminary thoughts on these topics.

Natural Law

Is what I have presented in this work a 'new natural law' theory?[10] At times, ecologically oriented legal theory has been merged with the anthropocentric and even the theocentric traditions of natural law,[11] without interrogating the vast difference between the constructions of human nature that inform natural law thought and of nature understood as the primarily nonhuman physical world. As discussed in Chapter 2, in the theoretical traditions of the west, nature is either human or not human, either inherent or objectified. Is it possible to wrest the idea of 'nature' away from a 'human nature' of intrinsic rationality and at the same time to refuse the distinction between nature and human society-culture? Is it possible for something called 'natural law' to be qualitatively plural, place-located, emergent, and transitional? Such a move would involve aligning a concept of 'natural law' with the emergent form of normativity I have considered, which stands in contrast to the idea of objective and universal normativity usually associated with natural law. Undoubtedly, with a significant effort to re-define natural law, bringing into play both the intrinsic and extrinsic meanings of 'nature', such a thing is possible. But it is complicated by ingrained meanings and traditions, and therefore I would hesitate to use the term 'natural law' for my endeavour. But it is nonetheless important to consider what 'natural law' means in this context.

Natural law theory has promoted the view that nature contains normative and moral guidance for human action and possibly for human law. Although secular versions are now growing in influence,[12] natural law thought has been strongly shaped by supernatural belief and religious traditions.[13] Like positivist thought, natural law theory proposes an idea of law detached

---

9 Such questions and variations on them have been asked repeatedly throughout the many pandemic Zoom sessions where I spoke about various parts of this work. I am grateful to the participants in those sessions for raising so many critical questions.

10 I am grateful to William MacNeil for asking whether my previous book was a 'techno-pagan' version of natural law. See MacNeil 2018.

11 See critique of Earth jurisprudence by Norman 2021, 72–74.

12 See collected essays in Crowe and Lee 2019b.

13 But for a recent approach that is consistent with both secular and religious traditions see Crowe 2019.

from the contingencies of both human society and from the physical world. Far from understanding 'nature' as highly variable and local expressions of biological and physical processes, natural law relies on the idea of a universal human nature. Thus natural law is grounded nowhere and said to exist everywhere, in the same form across time and space.[14] In this form, natural law is the antithesis of Mariana Valverde's chronotope. Traditional natural law does not define a specific coming together of space and time, a 'thickening' of space and time around a purpose or phenomena;[15] rather it abandons space and time as largely irrelevant to its claims of universality.

Despite its idiosyncratic scope, natural law theory does pose some helpful questions for the twenty-first-century era of legal theory. The question that inspired this book is whether nature is normative.[16] As I have endeavoured to show, when expanded beyond the view that there is a universal human nature to include the material-semiotic processes of life and nonlife, the question is vast and complex. Critical sub-questions are what 'nature' encompasses and what 'normative' means. This question and sub-questions have been a central focus of this book – I have taken an expansive view of both nature and normativity, meaning that any 'natural law' that I promote is quite at odds with how it is understood in the jurisprudential tradition.

As I have mentioned, constructions of *human* nature have provided the foundation for extremely variable philosophical approaches. In natural law theory, the nature of human beings is the reference point for understanding human goods and – from that basis – assessments of what is right for human action and for political and legal arrangements.[17] But this 'nature' is highly specific, neither embodied nor connected to the nonhuman world. It is an abstract set of properties, an inherence. One obvious question for natural law theory that emerges from this book is: why does 'nature' stop at humans when we are so evidently enmeshed in an extended physical (and 'natural') world? Why does the 'nature' of natural law theory even *start* with the human? On what basis, if any, can essential human nature be divided from our animal nature and from vegetal nature, not to mention a ubiquitous microbial nature? Is it actually possible to bracket the air, the soil, the energy, and the water that constitutes us as living beings? Are not pre-human beings, embedded in our evolutionary present, regarded as

---

14 Finnis 1980; for an approach to natural law that does not adopt such universalism see Crowe 2019. I have offered some comments on Crowe's approach in Davies 2019.

15 See Valverde 2015, 10.

16 Crowe 2019, 15.

17 Crowe and Lee 2019a.

integral to the 'nature' that is said to define us? Natural law theory will only live up to its name when it is embedded in the whole of nature and accepts the radically plural and complex (and hence emerging and non-objective) nature of nature.

As many writers have been insisting now for some decades, this severance of the human from the nonhuman is a construct of human (and largely western) thought: the human-nonhuman division is not itself a property of the world.[18] What *is* a property of the world is our co-existence with other beings. As animals, human beings are not simple individuals but rather composites characterized by symbiosis rather than by separation. As Scott Gilbert et al have said, in an article subtitled 'we have never been individuals', 'animals can no longer be considered individuals in any sense of classical biology: anatomical, developmental, physiological, immunological, genetic, or evolutionary'.[19] The human is a symbiotic being, distributed and networked, not a unit. We are 'biocultural creatures' to use Samantha Frost's term.[20] It might nonetheless be thought that the rest of nature, both living and nonliving, can be bracketed in a consideration of human law, but is that correct? If anything may be said to meet the standard of self-evidence, it is that humans belong to an extended physical nature and that therefore natural law theory is overdue a reorientation towards nature beyond the human. A secular natural law, after all, is not bound to the idea that human beings are made in the image of God: rather, we are a species of animal that has evolved as part of the extraordinary flourishing of life on earth. Starting with that natural diversity and symbiotic connectedness would yield quite different results for traditional natural law. The 'good of life', for instance, much discussed within natural law thought,[21] is more astonishing and far-reaching when we understand it in the light of symbiosis, than when we limit it to family, friends, and human reproductive capacity.[22] Can the distinction between nature as immanence and nature as the physical world be further dismantled by bringing the laws of nature *beyond* the human, for instance biological and geological processes, into the understanding of natural law?

---

18 Graham 2008; Plumwood 1993.
19 Gilbert et al 2012, 334. See also Krakauer et al 2020.
20 Frost 2016.
21 Finnis 1980, 86; Crowe 2019, 39–41. Catherine Carol 2019 provides a more grounded discussion of a related concept, a gendered 'good of generativity'.
22 It is also arguable that reproducing human life, at this point in human expansion, is doing as much harm as good – which is not to say that we should regard it as a human bad, but rather that its 'goodness' might be equivocal.

There are signs that within self-described natural law theory the idea of 'nature' is indeed being cautiously extended in this way.[23] To take one example, in his recent book, *Natural Law and the Nature of Law*, Jonathan Crowe presents a dynamic idea of natural law, which is partly informed by facts about human nature that change – notably biological facts that change with evolution and social facts that change with history.[24] Crowe takes some steps to narrow the divide between a purely abstract and idealized concept of immanent human nature and our existence in a physical world. In discussing the 'facts about human nature' that are part of the background of natural law, for instance, he frequently invokes evolution and biology as the infrastructure, along with society, that shapes human nature. 'My use of the term *human nature* is meant to encompass a range of natural facts about humans (roughly the kinds of facts that can be analysed by the natural and social sciences)'.[25] Thus, human biology is a central cause and a condition for natural law, according to Crowe, and to this degree, there is recognition of the physical world in his account of natural law, even though it remains anchored in human existence.

More ambitiously, 'Earth jurisprudence' claims the existence of a 'Great Law', translating natural law theory with its focus on individual human subjects to Earth and nonhuman subjects.[26] Universal rights of nature flow from the idea that natural entities are subjects of this Great Law.[27] In this view, human law is seen as either more or less aligned with the 'Great Law', much as classical natural law theory accepts the existence of separate spheres of human and natural law. Within the natural law tradition, Earth jurisprudence (or better, 'ecological jurisprudence'[28]) and Jonathan Crowe's reformulation of nature may open the way for natural law theory

---

23 Catherine Carol 2019, for instance, connects Irigaray's work on universal embodied sexual difference to natural law, while Michael Detmold 2019, 327 says: 'The state of nature that founds natural law . . . could be nothing else than the physical/biological state of affairs prior to the evolution of humans'. In both cases, however, the focal point of natural law remains human.

24 Crowe 2019.

25 Ibid, 117.

26 Berry 2006; Cullinan 2015; Burdon 2015; cf comments by Pelizzon and Ricketts 2015, who propose an 'ecological jurisprudence' as an advance on the Earth jurisprudence version of natural law theory, because it is not tied to the universals of natural law. See also Pelizzon 2020.

27 This emphasis on universality contrasts with contexts where rights of nature have been proposed as strategic or localized reforms, or as a way of bringing Indigenous concepts into dialogue with colonial law. See Tănăsescu 2020.

28 Pelizzon and Ricketts 2015.

to break free of anthropocentrism in the description of law and to become more expansive. But if this is to be achieved, the distinction between human and nonhuman will need to be thoroughly challenged.[29] But is this even an aspiration for *natural law* theory?

Positive Law in a Normative Pluriverse

The scope of 'nature' will undoubtedly remain contested but no more so than the scope of 'law'. The question remains how is it possible to describe and account for positive and limited law within the fields of normative plurality that I have explored. Legal positivism has become definitive of law in its dominant forms – when lawyers in Anglo and other European traditions speak of 'law', they still mostly assume the positivist lens. The mainstream popular idea of 'law' is also a positivist one – it claims that within any one nation-state there is only one set of institutions and practices capable of producing law and therefore only one law. For this reason, positivism poses two unavoidable challenges for any legal theory: first, theory has to *account for* positive law even if it does not confine itself to it as a definitive image of law; and second, there is the issue of the *law-ness of law*. What is the meaning of 'law' for legal theory? In many countries, a founding and ongoing political-epistemological-legal violence means that 'law' is taken to mean the law of the colonizers, a law that lacks the authority of place-emergent law.[30] This truth needs to sit underneath everything the colonial state calls 'law'.

At the same time, relationality means that *all* 'law', including the nation-state law imposed by colonialism, is connected in some way to that tree, the slime mould at its base, those butterflies, that honeyeater, this land, the river, those rocks. This is as true of human positive (imposed, colonial) law as it is of 'unofficial' law and the Indigenous knowledges of law that are – especially in Australia but also elsewhere – based on explicit connections between community, land, and 'nature' or ecosystems. Although I cannot fully unpack these connections and disconnections here, I can offer a few thoughts about where positive law sits politically and materially within the extended field of the plural *nomos* that I have described.

Those of us strongly inculcated in the liberal-colonial tradition are – slowly and sometimes reluctantly – learning that First Nations worlds are highly relational and that they each hold their own knowledges and

---

29 There are some aspirational and ultimately incomplete attempts to develop classical natural law into ecocentric natural law. See eg Berry 2006.
30 'The state has power derived from its original violent colonial foundation ... but it does not have the law-full authority'. Watson 2017, 210. See also Giannacopoulos 2021.

ontology of the cosmological and the local. These connected world views are routinely contrasted with the colonial world view, which are built upon a mythology of separation from nature and from place, as Martuwarra RiverOfLife et al explain:

> First Law is the way of living on Country handed down through countless generations. It sustains a web of relationships between the human and the non-human world and 'forms a pattern which is life itself.' This pattern must be recreated and the Law followed to sustain life. First Law is holistic and emphasizes the connections between the parts of the 'pattern' of life and the whole, and makes it clear that the whole is greater than the sum of its parts. Indigenous knowledge and legal systems consider reductionist world views to be fundamentally flawed. This is because the failure to understand connection leads to a failure to value those connections. This results in destruction for both the individual and the collective.[31]

Colonial law is based on a 'failure to understand connection', and it is critical that we (western legal theorists) start conceiving the things that have been mythologized as separate, including our 'law', as in fact connected.

In colonized places the idea that law is connected to the land and to ecosystems is not straightforward, for a few reasons. First, the liberal narrative of Anglo-centric law is based on there being a line between things that are regulated and things that are not, a zone of governance and the remaining outside, a zone of freedom and of things that are unaddressed by law. The default presumption is of legal disinterest in most nonhuman things as well as a large slab of human life. Second, when things are drawn into the zone of regulation, because of the objectifying processes of law, any 'connection' is formal, reduced, and two-dimensional. Nation-state law encodes the world as object, meaning that it reduces complexity and plenitude to only things that are of concern to state law, and only those aspects of those things that are seen to matter. However, this coding of physical things as object rather than subject is only one – politically imposed and culturally dominant – slice across the dense materiality that constitutes the normative world. As I have argued, even the law that is perceived as separate is nonetheless a product of multiple intersecting nonhuman (bio, geo, cosmo, eco) normativities.

---

31 Martuwarra RiverOfLife et al 2020, 546–547, quoting Kwaymullina and Kwaymullina 2010. See also Bawaka Country et al 2016.

Because of the entrenched narrative of separation, the 'connection' between the imposed law and land/ecosystems is often understood negatively: law is understood as exclusive of material life rather than based within it. That it is actually at once separated *and* connected provides a more complex narrative for theory. Like extractive capitalism, the ideology of nation-state law devalues the things that it is reliant on. The problem, as others have explained, is that the colonial legal-economic-social matrix is *perceived* as detached when it is not.[32] Its costs and connections are not visible because they are external to that which is designated as inside to law. For its part, law is perceived as essentially formal and conceptual and therefore as a neutral medium for governance. This neutrality is a strategic charade and hence often destructive – based as it is on objectification, alienation, a denial of connection, and a denial of the living meaningful beings of nonhuman others. Analogous arguments have been made for decades by feminists and critical race theorists, who have criticized the notion that law is a blindfolded medium and that areas of apparent legal non-interference are really 'free'.[33] Law's technical limits leave both the 'unregulated' free public sphere and the invisible domestic and private sphere largely aligned with values extracted from the male-dominated history of law and a Eurocentric patriarchal culture.

As things stand, the concepts, practices and above all institutional forms of the dominant legal system cannot be abandoned. This system is a critical component of the social glue protecting the so-called democracies of the west from authoritarianism and unchecked corruption. Positivism's value derives from its status as the fiction that enables legal analysis, doctrine, and practice in a certain context but it fails as a description of law – it unifies, singularizes, and systematizes where there is intrinsic plurality, lack of boundaries, complex relationships, and interpretations replete with social power and meaning. But there can also be no doubt that both the practice of this law and its concept are, as they always have been, in transition – at this time away from the image of self-containment that dominated the twentieth century towards a more socially connected image where, increasingly, the normative world includes plants, animals, ecosystems, and entities in the natural environment such as rivers and mountains.[34]

---

32 See, for instance, Graham 2011.
33 See eg Nunn 1997; O'Donovan 1985.
34 Geddis and Ruru 2020; Tomas 2011.

Self-Identity and Co-Becoming: Autopoiesis and Sympoiesis

I want to conclude this chapter by reflecting on these matters through the lens of the legal theoretical engagement with the concepts of autopoiesis and sympoiesis. These ideas offer biologically inspired framework for theorizing separability and self-organization on the one hand and interconnected co-becoming on the other. As I have endeavoured to argue in this book, both strategies are necessary to the emergence of legality.

Autopoiesis is a term invented by Humberto Maturano and Francisco Varela to describe the self-making capacity of living systems, typically the cell.[35] It is above all a view of life as system, as unity and as autonomous (self-regulating): an autopoietic system has boundaries, is perceptible as a single entity, and occupies a defined space. Its cognition is its own. Being a unity does not imply total closure – the cell has a highly permeable membrane.[36] But the cycling of stimuli and materials from outside is regulated by the system and used in its own self-construction.[37] A living system is differentiated from its outside by virtue of this self-regulation of boundary and of processes that maintain, alter, and reproduce the system. As mentioned in Chapter 3, Maturano and Varela insisted that living systems are machines: they have identity and autonomy but are not intrinsically purpose-driven – in Kantian style, teleonomy (or teleology) is 'only an artifice of . . . description'.[38]

Autopoiesis has been used extensively as an analogy for understanding social and legal systems. Autopoiesis focuses on the unity and self-containment of systems and has a powerful analogue in self-reproducing, bounded, legal systems.[39] The deployment of the idea of autopoiesis in sociology and law by Niklas Luhmann, Gunther Teubner, and others translated the qualities of the self-organizing cell into the context of law, emphasizing in particular that, as a system, 'law' (typically but not exclusively state law[40]) is self-constructing. As Luhmann put it: 'The unity of the system is produced by the system itself'.[41] Such a system is not empirically closed. But it maintains a boundary – a metaphorical cell membrane which is essentially a code – between legal norms and 'norms which are simply opinions in its

---

35 Maturana and Varela 1980.
36 See eg Frost 2016.
37 Maturana and Varela 1980, 82.
38 Ibid, 86.
39 Luhmann 1992; Teubner 1992; see generally the critique by Valverde 2006.
40 Teubner 1992, 1451 clearly indicates that there can be plural autopoietic legal systems.
41 Luhmann 1992, 1420.

environment'.[42] For legal theory, 'the problem is *how to define the operation that differentiates the system and organizes the difference between system and environment* while maintaining reciprocity between dependence and independence'.[43] In other words, theorists need to be able to define the system's boundary operations while allowing for connection between inside and outside that results in internal change that is autonomous. For law, the exercise in boundary construction and maintenance results in a binary code between legal and non-legal – as sole producer of legal norms, the system can always identify what is a legal norm and what is not. Whilst the legal system has 'highly selective connections'[44] with the outside environment, any inflow of information needs to be constructed internally before it is useful. In its legal applications, autopoiesis deploys an idealized and seemingly static spatiotemporal schema – there are insides and outsides to the legal system, and it changes in a linear fashion. It appears to be essentially momentary, with no logical or historical beginning, only self-conditioned reconstructions of its own history.[45]

The most notable difference between autopoiesis as an explanation of living systems and autopoiesis as a description of law concerns the nature of the topology as involving, in the case of life, biochemical matter and, in the case of law, communications. In biology, metabolic processes demand 'material openness':[46] the cell needs food from outside itself, which is transformed by its operations into energy and usable molecules, in order to perform its functions. Therefore environment-system is a material relation. Moreover, cellular topology describes a physical space with a permeable but defined boundary. By contrast, the legal autopoietic system excludes any reference to *material* exchange between the inside and outside of a system and does not occupy physical space.[47] Corporeal beings such as human

---

42 Ibid, 1427.
43 Ibid, 1426 (emphasis in original).
44 Ibid, 1432.
45 'Historically, there is no beginning except an always renewed reconstruction of the past. Logically, there are no apriorities, but simply a circular, reciprocal conditioning of the code and programs'. Ibid, 1428.
46 Maturana and Varela 1980, x.
47 As Philippopoulos-Mihalopoulos 2014, 396 explains, this does not mean that matter is absent from autopoietic theory of law. Rather, it is coded as extrinsic by the operations that define the system. Philippopoulos-Mihalopoulos re-reads Luhmann through new materialism, emphasizing that matter is always in the background of legal autopoiesis, even if it is not explicitly part of the autopoietic description of law. This means, to summarize crudely, that matter constantly intrudes in various ways and becomes part of the boundary of law. Despite this reading, it is unclear whether autopoietic theory of law can insist

bodies in their patterned social existences play no role in the description of an autopoietic legal system, even though such a system is unimaginable without them. The legal system understood through autopoiesis can define, organize, and govern space, but law's boundaries are not co-extensive with the physical boundaries of a legally defined territory or nation. Rather than deploy any material explanation, the autopoietic legal system is comprised of communications, programs, and coding.

The backgrounding of materiality and physicality limits the scope of autopoiesis as a description of law. Although it makes many useful points about the formally self-producing capacities of a legal system in the positivist modality, autopoiesis produces a singular, we might say two-dimensional and highly idealized, version of law, only applicable to 'systems' that can be conceptualized as closed (only on an abstract plane, therefore) and not to the multiple normativities that surround, hold up, overlap with, and subvert those systems. By contrast to this view, it is clear that in practice legal communication cannot be so easily dissociated from material processes and, in particular, from the human bodies that actively perform and produce the law.[48] The popularity of autopoiesis as an image of law has possibly declined with waning interest in explaining the unity and positivity of a legal system, and rising interest in understanding law's many material textures and socio-political entanglements.

Returning to *matter* in biological explanation offers other possibilities for understanding the identity of legal systems as a product of prior, and continuing, co-becoming. As mentioned in Chapter 3, in biology, autopoiesis has been supplemented with symbiosis and symbiogenesis[49] – the fact that life forms live and originate *with* one another. All life is symbiotic, in that we (all living beings) are physically dependent on other living beings. Moreover, life originates symbiogenetically, which is to say that differences or new forms of life are produced by interchanges between species or 'strains' rather than by random genetic mutations that occur 'within' an organism.[50] Co-becoming, rather than individual change, is fundamental. Extending these ideas – not just analogically but also literally – Donna Haraway has

---

upon operational closure when unfiltered matter so obviously disrupts the processes for self-replication of law.

48 For further explanation and discussion see Davies 2017b.

49 See eg Margulis 1967, 2010. Margulis had several Russian predecessors who were the first to theorize evolution by symbiosis rather than by random mutation. See Margulis 2001, 60–61.

50 Margulis 2001, 59.

theorized 'sympoiesis' as 'making together'.[51] Haraway's sympoiesis is not confined to the biological world, but is made of heterogeneous intellectual, activist, and artistic compostables: it includes the co-becoming of art, literature, biological beings, geo-things – in short, the multiplicities of being. As she says: 'If it is true that neither biology nor philosophy any longer supports the notion of independent organisms in environments, that is, interacting units plus contexts/rules, then sympoiesis is the name of the game in spades'.[52] The thought of sympoiesis – of co-becoming rather than autonomy – provides a more complex, less framed, orientation for theory that can encompass both the plurality of qualitatively different 'systems' and ongoing hybridization across these pluralities.

Adding the term 'sympoiesis' to the lexicon of law is a helpful reminder of several aspects of legal intra-activity. Anna Grear has coined the term 'sympoietic normativities' specifically to describe norms that emerge from human-nonhuman relationships, arguing that such normativities hold potential for 'grounding a renewing legal imaginary for the Anthropocene'.[53] Sympoietic normativities, she explains, are not 'ambitious and "overarching" aspirations for Earth System law/governance'.[54] In other words, they are not necessarily translatable – or at least not immediately and directly – into the grand law reform or regulatory efforts of nation-states. Rather, they are embedded in horizontal relational dynamics that engage a much broader legal imaginary than state law: Grear says sympoietic normativities might emerge from 'human-non-human working groups in a wide range of situated endeavours in commons-based, grassroots initiatives, expanded to embrace "commoners" who are more than simply-human'.[55] Sympoietic normativities can be *made* by a coming together of human and nonhuman: Grear says such norms 'could arise' and that they 'could hold out space for co-negotiation'.[56] These formulations suggest a deliberate effort to create new norms out of a dialogue or at least an engagement with nonhuman beings: 'Groups and communities (imagined as symbiont clusterings)

51 Haraway credits Beth Dempster with the first use of the term 'sympoiesis' in 1998. Haraway 2016, 33 quotes Dempster's master's thesis, which defined sympoiesis as 'collectively-producing systems that do not have self-defined spatial or temporal boundaries. Information and control are distributed among components. The systems are evolutionary and have the potential for surprising change'. See also Dempster 2000.

52 Haraway 2016, 33.

53 Grear 2020, 360.

54 Ibid, 361. See also Petersmann 2020 for a critique of the ontological commitments of Earth System law.

55 Ibid.

56 Ibid.

could form evolutive sympoietic partnerships across and between groups, generating new normative formations and praxes' (emphasis added).[57] Such human-promoted efforts to enter into imaginative partnerships with nonhuman realms are now even reasonably common – their normative or legal resonance might not always be foregrounded, but certainly the meanings and modes of co-becoming are routinely explored.[58] Grear's work therefore names the making of a new *nomos* that emerges through a recognition of sympoietic partnerships across the spectrum of life (and potentially non-life). It suggests deliberate coming together of human and nonhuman to create new normative spaces. Such normative co-becomings need to be *made* because current dominant constructions of law pay so little attention to the normative import of the physical world.

On another, more immanent, plane, normative co-becomings already exist because of the inevitable interaction of human and nonhuman normativities. Indeed, it seems reasonable to regard all normativity as sympoietic insofar as all normativity involves micro-cosmic chemistry, the symbiotic and symbiogenetic processes responsible for life, the co-becoming of self and *Umwelt*, a co-becoming with others, and the vast planes of human and nonhuman meaning making that emerge from these processes. Insofar as norms are the result of iterative actions, the material-semiotic other is always embedded in the process of norm creation. Thus, expanding the onto-epistemological frame of normativity to include a much wider range of relationships and fields of perception suggests that sympoietic normativity describes an *already existent* – and continuously emergent – normative becoming and co-becoming.[59] For this reason, Marie-Catherine Petersmann argues that an essentially unified and autopoietic 'Earth system law' is problematic: there can be no overarching or unified law to govern Earth because everything is contingent upon heterogeneous and non-unifiable sympoietic processes.[60]

In sum, 'sympoietic normativities' can be produced by deliberate acts of partnering between human and nonhuman, but must also be based in the inherent and immanent normativity (that is, the norm-creating properties) of our bio-relations.[61] Sympoiesis can point to the multiple heterogeneous strata and scales of normativity that are necessary if state law is to exist and

57 Ibid, 362.
58 See eg Robinson and Raven 2020; Turner and Somerville 2020; Niemanis 2009; Gibson 2020; Bradshaw 2020; Akhtar-Khavari 2020.
59 See eg Petersmann 2020.
60 Ibid.
61 See my comments in Chapter 1 regarding the 'natural contract' proposed by Serres.

operate.[62] But for the becoming-together of bodily, environmental, cultural, political (etc) registers of normativity, state law could not exist. Sympoiesis is moreover an apt term for the novel normative bonds that emerge when plural laws relate and hybridize.[63]

Conclusion

In different ways, the questions I have considered in this chapter are all variations on the (timeless, place-less, and indeed endless) theme of continuity and discontinuity. Natural law thought, even in its Earth-focused manifestations, has to date been constrained by its anthropocentrism, characterized in this instance as the foreclosure of nature beyond a presumed human essence. Natural law thought has failed to account both for the continuities between the human and the nonhuman and for the intrinsic normativity of the physical world, living and nonliving. State-based positive law is also defined by several conceptual discontinuities: from other such systems of law, from society, and from place-based emergent ecosocial *nomos*. These conceptual separations are in some senses critical to the functioning (good and bad) of 'law' as understood in this format. At the same time, such separations are neither conceptually possible nor materially defensible. 'Law' does not exist and cannot function without the extended normative pluriverse. Its relative stability and coherence remains a product of a much more expansive and disorderly materiality. And finally autopoiesis and sympoiesis/ symbiosis provide an interesting case study of the transplantation of biological language and thinking into the legal theoretical context. The biological processes of autopoiesis provide a metaphor for legal system autonomy. Symbiosis and sympoiesis can be understood metaphorically but also, more importantly, literally, as material co-becoming across every field of legality. In law as in biology sympoietic co-becoming is historically, materially, and conceptually fundamental – the unity of any law, such as it is, is contingent upon and situated within the normative, always emerging, pluralities that characterize life and nonlife on Earth.

---

62 Davies 2017a, 2017b.
63 Griffith 1998; Von Benda-Beckman and Turner 2018; Melissaris 2009.

Conclusion

The vision of a singular world in which there can be only one reality, one model human being, one law, one world, and one truth may work for a few, but not for most, humans, and not at all for the objectified nonhuman world. As I have outlined in the previous chapters, the ecological reorientation of thought means starting with connection rather than with the fixed taxonomies of modernist thought. The emphasis on connection and relationality is a challenge in the first instance to the familiar dualisms of the modern era, which are political as well as epistemological. Distinctions that are ontologically problematic include those routinely made between nature and culture, reason and emotion, subject and object, mind and body, fact and norm, being and becoming, as well as many others. The political character of these modes of thought arises from their contingent yet stubbornly resilient alignment with social hierarchies and distributions of power.

The critique of these dualisms has often been deconstructive – showing how the terms are produced discursively and that they are held apart yet entangled by the political operations of language. Law and nature, for instance, can be deconstructed as cultural-linguistic operators, a move that shows the fictive character and the contingency of the distinction. The focus on connection stems from a different theoretical strategy that points to material processes. Therefore, I have considered the ontological continuity of norm-creating processes across human and nonhuman, living and nonliving. But in taking this approach, I have emphasized a minor slice of western philosophy that builds upon scientific engagement with the physical world. This represents only one of many possible engagements with the law-nature problematic, which is primarily situated within the cultural horizon of Eurocentrism. It proposes a provisional concept of normativity that is in one sense unlimited because it appears across emergent formations of matter. But my analysis is entirely limited nonetheless and sidelines some significant angles including many

DOI: 10.4324/9781003128335-7

of which Indigenous peoples have longstanding and secure knowledge: these include the place-based nature of normative worlds, the ethics of law, and the non-physical (some would say sacred or spiritual) dimensions of legal commitments.

Because of the brevity of this book, and also because of the limited task I set myself, I have made few attempts to thicken this account of normativity with situated detail. This limitation lends problematic universality to my account and possibly aligns me more closely than I would otherwise like to mainstream jurisprudence. In much legal theory, especially throughout the twentieth century, the commitment to a generalizable description of law that works for all times and all places has been strong and has underpinned the nature-culture distinction. Laws might vary according to time and place, but the form or *concept* of law remains the same, in this view. Legal positivism promotes a singular concept that allows law to be transported from place to place and only adapted locally from an original model: for instance, and despite its highly localized beginnings, under colonial conditions the English common law was understood to be capable of movement with English subjects as their birthright, according to Blackstone.[1] Because the law could be uprooted, it was understood as dissociated from its location. In consequence and as outlined above, this idea about law became entirely detached from human social networks, from its economic and historical conditions, and most significantly from ecological connections in specific places. This Eurocentric commitment to the universal is now contested by plurality in not only the content of law but also its form and conceptualization. The experience of law, like all experience, is pluriversal (or even fractiversal[2]) rather than universal. Law shares its plurality with other facets of human socio-cultural being, as well as with nature,[3] and even with physical reality as understood by mainstream scientists. The world we inhabit is one of plural pluralities and plural normativities, that intersect but are differentiated by vectors such as culture, place, experience, politics, and existential outlook.[4]

The theoretical developments that I have discussed in this book suggest above all an image of normative multiplicity and complexity across intersecting but unaligned fields or sectors of existence. There is no closure to be found anywhere among these normative pluralities as they are all

---

1 Blackstone 1765, 107; see also Davies 2020.
2 Law 2015; Aston 2020.
3 De la Cadena and Blaser 2018.
4 Davies 2017b.

interrelated: closure, as we know, is a myth and/or a type of violence. And nor can anything quite stay in place, where it was before. As Annemarie Mol says, discussing Canguilhem's essay on the connection of biological and social normativity,

> If there is no single norm to orient normalization, if instead there are several plausible but different norms which do not cohere but exist in tension, *society* does not stay the same. . . . it may be that 'society' is over. Not because there are only individuals and families left, but rather because the fleshy, financial, metal and fluid matters that constitute it, form tense, multivocal, non-organic patterns for which the words are still to be invented.[5]

'Society' as a singular body may be over, but 'societies' as plural human-nonhuman relationships and regularities abound. The possibilities for inventing new words that name the normative continuities, hybridities, and interruptions across these multiple normative planes are considerable. However, this has not been my intention in this book. More prosaically and perhaps paradoxically, I have been motivated by the need to consider some slightly mechanical questions – what do (some of) these normative fields consist of, how are they composed, and how can we understand the continuities and discontinuities between human (especially state) law and a *nomos* that extends well beyond a limited human domain to everything else in existence?

It is in one sense inevitable that *legal* theory needs to account for positive law and also, as a practical matter, to mobilize it as a strategy for reform in the expectation that over time it is itself transformed by its many small interventions.[6] Twenty-first century commentary also grasps the need for new legal imaginaries of normative complexity, plurality, and continuity between all earthly phenomena.[7] As I have noted repeatedly throughout this book, such efforts to comprehend human and nonhuman within a common legal theoretical frame have been motivated and guided by First Nations world views about the embeddedness of law in land-community relations, but there are literally oceans and millennia, not to mention a myriad of social factors, dividing western legal thought from good

---

5 Mol 1998, 284.
6 See eg Pelizzon and Ricketts 2015.
7 Ibid; see also Akhtar-Khavari 2020; Philippopoulos-Mihalopoulos 2014; Grear 2020; Petersmann 2021.

comprehension of these truths.[8] Careful attention to Indigenous voices and thoughtful cross-disciplinary constructions are slowly beginning to produce a body of scholarship in which located human and nonhuman are partners, in dialogue, and mutually reliant. A significant project for scholars whose primary location has been the western intellectual tradition is therefore to cultivate an attitude that listens and engages imaginatively and openly with First Nations ontologies.[9] Many of us who live on colonized land now regard this as both an ethical imperative and a profound critical challenge to everyday scholarly narratives.

---

8 Cf Bawaka Country et al 2016; Martuwarra RiverOfLife et al 2020; Watson 2000; Kway-mullina and Kwaymullina 2010.
9 Anker 2017; Hamilton and Neimanis 2018; Verran 2018; T O'Donnell et al 2020; Wright 2020.

References

Adamatsky, Andrew ed 2016 *Advances in Physarum Machines: Sensing and Computing with Slime Mould*, Springer

Ahmed, Sara 2006 *Queer Phenomenology: Orientations, Objects, Others*, Duke University Press

Ahmed, Sarah 2008 'Some Preliminary Remarks on the Founding Gestures of the "New Materialism"' *European Journal of Women's Studies* 15(1): 23–39

Akhtar-Khavari, Afshin 2020 'Restoration and Co-operation for Flourishing Socio-Ecological Landscapes' *Transnational Legal Theory* 11(1–2): 62–74

Allchin and Werth 2020 'How We Think About Human Nature: The Naturalizing Error' *Philosophy of Science* 87: 499–517

Allen, Garland 2005 'Mechanism, Vitalism, and Organicism in Late Nineteenth and Twentieth-Century Biology: The Importance of Historical Context' *Studies in History and Philosophy of Biological and Biomedical Sciences* 36: 261–283

Allison, Henry 1991 'Kant's Antinomy of Teleological Judgment' *Southern Journal of Philosophy* 30(supp): 25–42

Althusser, Louis 1994 'Ideology and Ideological State Apparatuses' in Slavoj Zizek ed *Mapping Ideology*, Verso

Anker, Kirsten 2017 'Law as . . . Forest: Eco-Logic, Stories and Spirits in Indigenous Jurisprudence' *Law Text Culture* 21: 191–213

Aristotle 1984a 'Metaphysics' in WD Ross trans, Jonathan Barnes ed *The Complete Works of Aristotle Volume 2: The Revised Oxford Translation*, Princeton University Press

Aristotle 1984b 'Physics', in RP Hardie and RK Gaye trans, Jonathan Barnes ed *The Complete Works of Aristotle Volume 1: The Revised Oxford Translation*, Princeton University Press

Aristotle 1997 *The Politics*, Peter L Phillips Simpson trans, University of North Carolina Press

Arup, Gustav Stenseke 2021 *Entangled: A Study of the Entanglement of Wolves, Humans, and Law in the Landscape*, Karlstad University Studies

Asma, Stephen 2018 'Teleology Rises from the Grave' *Philosophy Now* 126: 20–23

Aston, Rhys 2020 *Inviting New Worlds: Jurisgenesis, Anarchism, and Prefigurative Social Change*, PhD Dissertation, Flinders University

Aston, Rhys and Margaret Davies 2022 forthcoming 'Ground(s)' in Daniela Gandorfer and Peter Goodrich eds *Research Handbook in Law and Literature*, Edward Elgar

Austin, John 1954 *The Province of Jurisprudence Determined*, Weidenfeld and Nicholson

Bailey, Cyril 1947 *Titi Lucreti Cari De Rerum Natura Libri Sex, Edited with Prolegomena, Critical Apparatus, Translation and Commentary*, Volume II Commentary, Books I–III, Clarendon Press

Barad, Karen 2007 *Meeting the Universe Halfway: Quantum Physics and the Entanglement of Matter and Meaning*, Duke University Press

Barad, Karen 2010 'Quantum Entanglements and Hauntological Relations of Inheritance: Dis/continuities, SpaceTime Enfoldings, and Justice-to-Come' *Derrida Today* 3: 240–268

Barad, Karen 2012 'On Touching – The Inhuman That Therefore I Am' *Differences: A Journal of Feminist Cultural Studies* 23(3): 206–223.

Barham, James 2012 'Normativity, Agency, and Life' *Studies in History and Philosophy of Biological and Biomedical Sciences* 43: 92–103

Barr, Olivia 2016 *Jurisprudence of Movement: Common Law, Walking, Unsettling Place*, Routledge

Barthes, Roland 1972 *Mythologies*, Annette Lavers trans, Jonathan Cape

Bartel, Robyn 2017 'Place-Thinking: The Hidden Geography of Environmental Law' in Andreas Philippopoulos-Mihalopoulos and Victoria Brooks eds *Research Methods in Environmental Law*, Edward Elgar

Bartel, Robyn 2018 'Place-Speaking: Attending to the Relational, Material, and Governance Messages of Silent Spring' *Geographical Journal* 184: 64–74

Bartel, Robyn and Nicole Graham 2016 'Property and Place Attachment: A Legal Geographical Analysis of Biodiversity Law Reform in New South Wales' *Geographical Research* 54(3): 267–284

Bawaka Country et al 2016 Co-Becoming Bawaka: Towards a Relational Understanding of Space/Place' *Progress in Human Geography* 40(4): 455–475

Beekman, Madeleine and Tanya Latty 2015 'Brainless but Multi-Headed: Decision-Making by the Acellular Slime Mould Physarum polycephalum' *Journal of Molecular Biology* 427: 3734–3743

Bennett, Jane 2010 *Vibrant Matter: A Political Ecology of Things*, Duke University Press

Bennett, Peter 1989 *Organic Gardening*, 5th ed, National Books

Bernasconi, Robert 2003 'Will the Real Kant Please Stand Up? The Challenge of Enlightenment Racism to the Study of the History of Philosophy' *Radical Philosophy* 117: 13–22

Bernstein, Jay 2019 'Introduction' in Millay Hyatt trans, Helmuth Plessner ed *Levels of Organic Life and the Human: An Introduction to Philosophical Anthropology*, Fordham University Press

Berry, Thomas 2006 *Evening Thoughts: Reflecting on Earth as a Sacred Community*, Sierra Club Books

Bickhard, Mark 2004 'Process and Emergence: Normative Function and Representation' *Axiomathes* 14: 121–155

Birrell, Kathleen and Daniel Matthews 2020 'Re-Storying Laws for the Anthropocene: Rights, Obligations, and an Ethics of Encounter' *Law and Critique* 31: 275–292

Blackstone, William 1765 *Commentaries on the Laws of England*, Volume 1, Clarendon Press

Blomley, Nicholas 2003 'From "What?" to "So What?": Law and Geography in Retrospect' in Jane Holder and Carolyn Harrison eds *Law and Geography: Current Legal Issues*, Oxford University Press

Blomley, Nicholas 2011 *Rights of Passage: Sidewalks and the Regulation of Public Flow*, Routledge

Blomley, Nicholas 2013 'Performing Property: Making the World' *Canadian Journal of Law and Jurisprudence* 26: 23–48

Blomley, Nicholas, David Delaney and Richard Ford eds 2001 *The Legal Geographies Reader*, Blackwell

Boelens, Rutgerd et al 2016 'Hydrosocial Territories: A Political Ecology Perspective' *Water International* 41: 1–14

Bordo, Susan 1986 'The Cartesian Masculinization of Thought' *Signs* 11(3): 439–456

Bowie, Andrew 2020 'Friedrich Wilhelm Joseph von Schelling' in Edward N Zalta ed *Stanford Encyclopedia of Philosophy*, Metaphysics Research Lab, https://plato.stanford.edu/archives/sum2020/entries/schelling/

Bradshaw, Karen 2020 *Wildlife as Property Owners: A New Conception of Animal Rights*, Chicago University Press

Braund, Edward, Raymond Sparrow and Eduardo Miranda 2016 'Physarum-Based Memristors for Computer Music' in Andrew Adamatsky ed *Advances in Physarum Machines: Sensing and Computing with Slime Mould*, Springer

Braverman, Irus, Nicholas Blomley, David Delaney and Alexandre Kedar eds 2014 *The Expanding Spaces of Law: A Timely Legal Geography*, Stanford University Press

Braverman, Irus and Elizabeth Johnson eds 2020 *Blue Legalities: The Life and Laws of the Sea*, Duke University Press

Breitenbach, Angela 2008 'Two Views on Nature: A Solution to Kant's Antinomy of Mechanism and Teleology' *British Journal for the History of Philosophy* 16(2): 351–369

Brooks, Victoria and Andreas Philippopoulos-Mihalopoulos eds 2017 *Research Methods in Environmental Law: A Handbook*, Edward Elgar

Burchett, Joseph et al 2020 'Revealing the Dark Threads of the Cosmic Web' *Astrophysical Journal Letters* 891(2): 1–12, https://doi.org/10.3847/2041-8213/ab700c

Burdon, Peter 2015 *Earth Jurisprudence: Private Property and the Environment*, Routledge

Butler, Judith 1990 *Gender Trouble: Feminism and the Subversion of Identity*, Routledge

Butler, Judith 1993 *Bodies That Matter: On the Discursive Limits of 'Sex'*, Routledge

Cahoone, Lawrence 2013 'The Irreducibility of Life to Mentality: Biosemiotics or Emergence?' in Brian G Henning and Adam Scarfe eds *Beyond Mechanism: Putting Life Back into Biology*, Lexington Books

Canguilhem, Georges 1978 *On the Normal and the Pathological*, first published 1966, D Reidel

Canguilhem, Georges 2008 *Knowledge of Life*, first published 1965, Stefanos Geroulanos and Daniela Ginsburg trans, Fordham University Press

Carlisle, Erin 2017 'On the Possibilities of Political Action in-the-World: Pathways Through Arendt, Castoriadis, and Wagner' *Social Imaginaries* 3(1): 83–118

Carol, Catherine 2019 'Luce Irigaray on Women and Natural Law' in Jonathan Crowe and Constance Youngwon Lee eds *Research Handbook on Natural Law Theory*, Edward Elgar

Caygill, Howard 2007 'Soul and Cosmos in Kant: A Commentary on "Two Things Fill the Mind. . ." in D Morgan et al eds *Cosmopolitics and the Emergence of a Future*, Palgrave Macmillan

Clark, Cristy, Nia Emmanouil, John Page, and Alessandro Pelizzon 2019 'Can You Hear the Rivers Sing? Legal Personhood, Ontology, and the Nitty-Gritty of Governance' *Ecology Law Quarterly* 45: 787–844

Clark, Cristy and John Page 2019 'Of Protest, the Commons, and Customary Public Rights: An Ancient Tale of the Lawful Forest' *UNSW Law Journal* 42(1): 26–59

Clark, Nigel and Myra Hird 2013 'Deep Shit' *O-Zone: A Journal of Object-Oriented Studies* 1: 44–52

Cleland, Carol 2019 *The Quest for a Universal Theory of Life*, Cambridge University Press

Code, Lorraine 1996 'What is Natural about Epistemology Naturalized?' *American Philosophical Quarterly* 33(1): 1–22

Code, Lorraine 2006 *Ecological Thinking: The Politics of Epistemic Location*, Oxford University Press

Cover, Robert 1983 'Nomos and Narrative' *Harvard Law Review* 97: 4–68

Coward, Rosalind and John Ellis 1977 *Language and Materialism: Developments in Semiology and the Theory of the Subject*, Routledge and Kegan Paul

Crowe, Jonathan 2019 *Natural Law and the Nature of Law*, Cambridge University Press

Crowe, Jonathan and Constance Youngwon Lee 2019a 'The Natural Law Outlook' in Jonathan Crowe and Constance Youngwon Lee eds *Research Handbook on Natural Law Theory*, Edward Elgar

Crowe, Jonathan and Constance Youngwon Lee eds 2019b *Research Handbook on Natural Law Theory*, Edward Elgar

Cullinan, Cormac 2015 *Wild Law: A Manifesto for Earth Justice*, 2nd ed, Green Books

Darwin, Charles 1906 *The Origin of Species*, first published 1859, John Murray

Davies, Margaret 1992 'Pathfinding: The Way of the Law' *Oxford Literary Review* 14: 107–131

Davies, Margaret 2015 'The Consciousness of Trees' *Law and Literature* 27(2): 217–235

Davies, Margaret 2016 'Material Subjects and Vital Objects – Prefiguring Property and Rights for an Entangled World' *Australian Journal of Human Rights* 22: 37–60

Davies, Margaret 2017a 'Plural Pluralities of Law' in Nicole Roughan and Andrew Halpin eds *In Pursuit of Pluralist Jurisprudence*, Cambridge University Press

Davies, Margaret 2017b *Law Unlimited: Materialism and Pluralism in Legal Theory*, Routledge

Davies, Margaret 2019 'The Time, Nature, and Place of Natural Law' *Australasian Journal of Legal Philosophy* 44: 106–116

Davies, Margaret 2020 'Distributed Cognition, Distributed Being, and the Foundations of Law' in Marc de Leeuw and Sonja van Wichelen eds *Personhood in the Age of Biolegality: Brave New Law*, Palgrave Macmillan

De la Cadena, Marisol and Mario Blaser eds 2018 *A World of Many Worlds*, Duke University Press

De Landa, Manuel 2000 *A Thousand Years of Nonlinear History*, Zone Books

Delaney, David 2010 *The Spatial, the Legal and the Pragmatics of World-Making: Nomospheric Investigations*, Routledge

De Leeuw, Marc and Sonja van Wichelin 2020 'Legal Personhood in Postgenomic Times: Plasticity, Rights, and Relationality' in Marc de Leeuw and Sonja van Wichelen eds *Personhood in the Age of Biolegality: Brave New Law*, Palgrave Macmillan

Deleuze, Gilles and Felix Guattari 1987 *A Thousand Plateaus: Capitalism and Schizophrenia*, Brian Massumi trans, University of Minnesota Press

Deleuze, Gilles and Felix Guattari 1994 *What Is Philosophy?*, Graham Burchell and Hugh Tomlinson trans, Verso

Dempster, Beth 2000 'Sympoietic and Autopoietic Systems: A New Distinction for Self-Organizing Systems' in JK Allen and J Wilby eds *Proceedings of the World Congress of the Systems Sciences*, ISSS

Derrida, Jacques 1981a *Dissemination*, Barbara Johnson trans, University of Chicago Press

Derrida, Jacques 1981b *Positions*, Alan Bass trans, University of Chicago Press

Derrida, Jacques 1988 *Limited Inc*, Samuel Weber trans, Northwestern University Press

Descartes, René 1982 *Principles of Philosophy*, first published 1644, Valentine Rodger Miller and Reese P Miller trans, Kluwer Academic Publishers

Des Chene, Dennis 1996 *Physiologia: Natural Philosophy in Late Aristotelianism and Cartesian Thought*, Cornell University Press

Des Chene, Dennis 2005 'Mechanisms of Life in the Seventeenth Century: Borelli, Perrault, Régis' *Studies in History and Philosophy of Biological and Biomedical Sciences* 36: 245–260

Detmold, Michael 2019 'Natural Law and Physics: The State of Nature' in Jonathan Crowe and Constance Youngwon Lee eds *Research Handbook on Natural Law Theory*, Edward Elgar

De Waal, Franz 2014 'Natural Normativity: The "Is" and "Ought" of Animal Behaviour' *Behaviour* 151: 185–204

Diaz, Sandra et al 2019 *Summary for Policymakers of the Global Assessment Report on Biodiversity and Ecosystem Services of the Intergovernmental Science-Policy Platform on Biodiversity and Ecosystem Services*, Intergovernmental Science-Policy Platform on Biodiversity and Ecosystem Services

Doyon, Maxim and Thiemo Breyer eds 2015 *Normativity in Perception*, Palgrave Macmillan

Dugatkin, Lee Alan 2011 *The Prince of Evolution*, Createspace

Dupré, John 2013 'Living Causes' *Proceedings of the Aristotelian Society* S87: 19–37

Duxbury, Neil 2017 'Custom as Law in English Law' *Cambridge Law Journal* 76: 337–359

Ehrlich, Eugen 1962 *Fundamental Principles of the Sociology of Law*, Walter Moll trans, Russell and Russell

Eichenseer, Kilian, Uwe Balthasar, Christopher W Smart, Julian Stander, Kristian A Haaga, and Wolfgang Kiessling 2019 'Jurassic Shift from Abiotic to Biotic Control on Marine Ecological Success' *Nature Geoscience* 12: 638–642

Ewick, Patricia and Susan Silbey 1998 *The Common Place of Law*, University of Chicago Press

Falcon, Andrea 2019 'Aristotle on Causality' in Edward N Zalta ed *The Stanford Encyclopedia of Philosophy*, Metaphysics Research Lab, https://plato.stanford.edu/archives/spr2019/entries/aristotle-causality/

Falk Moore, Sally 1973 'Law and Social Change: The Semi-Autonomous Social Field as an Appropriate Subject of Study' *Law and Society Review* 7: 719–746

Ferreira, Maria Isabel Aldinhas and Miguel Gama Caldas 2013 'The Concept of Umwelt Overlap and Its Application to Co-operative Action in Multi-Agent Systems' *Biosemiotics* 6: 497–514

Fiedler, K, B Hölldobler and P Seuffert 1996 'Butterflies and Ants: The Communicative Domain' *Experientia* 52: 14–24

Finchett-Maddock, Lucy 2017 'Speculative Entropy: Dynamism, Hyperchaos and the Fourth Dimension in Environmental Law Practice' in Victoria Brooks and Andreas Philippopoulos-Mihalopoulos eds *Research Methods in Environmental Law: A Handbook*, Edward Elgar

Finnis, John 1980 *Natural Law and Natural Rights*, Clarendon Press

Forster, Michael 2019 'Johann Gottfried von Herder' in Edward N Zalta ed *The Stanford Encyclopedia of Philosophy*, Metaphysics Research Lab, https://plato.stanford.edu/archives/sum2019/entries/herder/

Foucault, Michel 1967 *Madness and Civilization: A History of Insanity in the Age of Reason*, Tavistock

Fox Keller, Evelyn 2007a 'The Disappearance of Function from "Self-Organizing Systems"' in FC Boogerd et al eds *Systems Biology: Philosophical Foundations*, Elsevier

Fox Keller, Evelyn 2007b 'Slime Mold' in Sherry Turkle ed *Evocative Objects: Things We Think With*, MIT Press

Frenkel-Pinter, Moran et al 2021 'Water and Life: The Medium Is the Message' *Journal of Molecular Evolution* 89: 2–11

Frost, Samantha 2016 *Biocultural Creatures: Toward a New Theory of the Human*, Duke University Press

Gagliano, Monica 2018a 'Inside the Vegetal Mind: On the Cognitive Abilities of Plants' in Frantisek Baluska, Monica Gagliano, Guenther Witzany eds *Memory and Learning in Plants*, Springer

Gagliano, Monica 2018b *Thus Spoke the Plant: A Remarkable Journey of Groundbreaking Scientific Discoveries and Personal Encounters with Plants*, North Atlantic Books

Garber, Daniel and Sophie Roux eds 2013 *The Mechanization of Natural Philosophy*, Springer

Geddis, Andrew and Jacinta Ruru 2020 'Places as Persons: Creating a Legal Framework for Maori – Crown Relations' in Jason Varuhas ed *The Frontiers of Public Law*, Hart Publishing

Genel, Katia 2021 'The Norm, the Normal and the Pathological: Articulating Honneth's Account of Normativity with a French Account of the Norm (Foucault and Canguilhem)' *Critical Horizons* 22(1): 70–88

Giannacopoulos, Maria 2021 'White Law/Black Deaths: Nomocide and the Foundational Absence of Consent in Australian Law' *Australian Feminist Law Journal*, https://doi.org/10.1080/13200968.2021.1959994

Gibson, Johanna 2020 *Owned, an Ethological Jurisprudence of Property: From the Cave to the Commons*, Routledge

Gilbert, Scott, Jan Sapp and Alfred Tauber 2012 'A Symbiotic View of Life: We Have Never Been Individuals' *Quarterly Review of Biology* 87(4): 325–341

Ginsborg, Hannah 2001 'Kant on Understanding Organisms as Natural Purposes' in Eric Watkins ed *Kant and the Sciences*, Oxford University Press

Ginsborg, Hannah 2019 'Kant's Aesthetics and Teleology' in Edward N Zalta ed *The Stanford Encyclopedia of Philosophy*, Metaphysics Research Lab, https://plato.stanford.edu/archives/win2019/entries/kant-aesthetics/

Glennan, Stuart 2010 'Mechanisms, Causes, and the Layered Model of the World' *Philosophy and Phenomenological Research* 82(2): 362–381

Glennan, Stuart and Phyllis Illari eds 2018 *The Routledge Handbook of Mechanisms and Mechanistic Philosophy*, Routledge

Gotthelf, Allan 2012 *Teleology, First Principles, and Scientific Method in Aristotle's Biology*, Oxford University Press

Gould, Stephen Jay 1988 'Kropotkin Was No Crackpot' *Natural History* 97(7): 12–21

Grabham, Emily 2016 *Brewing Legal Times: Things, Form, and the Enactment of Law*, University of Toronto Press

Graham, Mary 2008 'Some Thoughts About the Philosophical Underpinnings of Aboriginal World Views' *Australian Humanities Review* 45: 181–194

Graham, Nicole 2011 *Lawscape: Property, Environment, Law*, Routledge

Grant, Iain Hamilton 2006 *Philosophies of Nature After Schelling*, Continuum

Grbich, Judith 1992 'The Body in Legal Theory' *University of Tasmania Law Review* 11: 26–58

Grear, Anna 2020 'Legal Imaginaries and the Anthropocene: "Of" and "For"' *Law and Critique* 31: 351–366

Greco, Monica 1998 'Between Social and Organic Norms: Reading Canguilhem and "Somatization"' *Economy and Society* 27(2–3): 234–248

Grene, Marjorie 1974 *The Understanding of Nature: Essays in the Philosophy of Biology*, D Riedel

Griffiths, Anne 1998 'Reconfiguring Law: An Ethnographic Perspective from Botswana' *Law and Social Inquiry* 23: 587–620

Grosz, Elizabeth 2004 *The Nick of Time: Politics, Evolution, and the Untimely*, Allen and Unwin

Grosz, Elizabeth, Kathryn Yusoff and Nigel Clark 2017 'An Interview with Elizabeth Grosz: Geopower, Inhumanism and the Biopolitical' *Theory, Culture, and Society* 34: 129–146

Hale, Matthew 1971 *History of the Common Law of England*, first published 1778, Charles Gray ed, University of Chicago Press

Hamilton, Jennifer Mae and Astrida Neimanis 2018 'Composting Feminisms and Environmental Humanities' *Environmental Humanities* 10(2): 501–527

Haraway, Donna 1988 'Situated Knowledges: The Science Question in Feminism and the Privilege of Partial Perspective' *Feminist Studies* 14(3): 575–599

Haraway, Donna 2003 *The Companion Species Manifesto*, Prickly Pear Press

Haraway, Donna 2016 *Staying with the Trouble: Making Kin in the Chthulucene*, Duke University Press

Hennig, Boris 2011 'Teleonomy' in Dominik Perler and Stephan Schmid eds *Final Causes and Teleological Explanation*, Brill

Henning, Brian G and Adam Scarfe eds 2013 *Beyond Mechanism: Putting Life Back into Biology*, Lexington Books

Hird, Myra 2006 'Animal Transex' *Australian Feminist Law Journal* 21(49): 35–50

Hird, Myra 2009 *The Origins of Sociable Life: Evolution After Science Studies*, Palgrave Macmillan

Hodder, Ian 2012 *Entangled: An Archaeology of the Relationships Between Humans and Things*, Wiley-Blackwell

Hoffman, Donald 2019 *The Case Against Reality: How Evolution Hid the Truth from Our Eyes*, Penguin

Hume, David 1969 *A Treatise of Human Nature*, first published 1740, Penguin

Jantsch, Erich 1980 *The Self-Organizing Universe: Scientific and Human Implications of the Emerging Paradigm of Evolution*, Pergamon

Joyce, Richard 2014 'The Origins of Moral Judgment' *Behaviour* 151: 261–278

Kabeshkin, Anton 2017 'Schelling on Understanding Organisms' *British Journal for the History of Philosophy* 25(6): 1180–1201

Kant, Immanuel 1929 *Critique of Pure Reason*, first published 1781, Norman Kemp Smith trans, Macmillan

Kant, Immanuel 1952 *Critique of Judgement*, first published 1790, James Creed Meredith trans, Clarendon Press

Kant, Immanuel 1993 *Critique of Practical Reason*, first published 1788, Lewis White Beck trans, Macmillan Publishing

Karpouzoglou, Timothy and Sumit Vij 2017 'Waterscape: A Perspective for Understanding the Contested Geography of Water' *WIREs Water* 4(3): 1–5

Kauffmann, Stuart A 2013 'Foreword' in Brian G Henning and Adam Scarfe eds *Beyond Mechanism: Putting Life Back into Biology*, Lexington Books

Kelsen, Hans 1967 *Pure Theory of Law*, Max Knight trans, University of California Press

Kelsen, Hans 1991 *General Theory of Norms*, Michael Hartney trans, Clarendon Press

Kerruish, Valerie 1983 'Philosophical Retreat: A Criticism of John Finnis' Theory of Natural Law' *University of Western Australia Law Review* 15: 224–244

Kotzé, Louis 2019 'Earth System Law for the Anthropocene' *Sustainability* 11: 6796, https://doi.org/10.3390/su11236796

Kotzé, Louis 2020 'Earth System Law for the Anthropocene: Rethinking Environmental Law Alongside the Earth System Metaphor' *Transnational Legal Theory* 11: 75–104

Kotzé, Louis and Rakhyun Kim 2019 'Earth System Law: The Juridical Dimensions of Earth System Governance' *Earth System Governance* 1: 100003, https://doi.org/10.1016/j.esg.2019.100003

Krakauer, D et al 2020 "The Information Theory of Individuality' *Theory in Biosciences* 139: 209–223

Kropotkin, Peter 1902 *Mutual Aid: A Factor of Evolution*, McClure Phillips & Co

Kwaymullina, Amber and Blaze Kwaymullina 2010 'Learning to Read the Signs: Law in an Indigenous Reality' *Journal of Australian Studies* 34(2): 195–208

Landecker, Hannah and Aaron Panofsky 2013 'From Social Structure and Gene Regulation and Back: A Critical Introduction to Environmental Epigenetics for Sociology' *Annual Review of Sociology* 39: 333–357

Langton, Marcia 2006 'Earth, Wind, Fire and Water: The Social Construction of Water in Aboriginal Societies' in Bruno David and Bryce Barker eds *The Social Archaeology of Australian Indigenous Societies*, AIATSIS

Lappé, Martine and Hannah Landecker 2015 'How the Genome Got a Lifespan' *New Genetics and Society* 34: 152–176

Latour, Bruno 2004 'Why Has Critique Run Out of Steam? From Matters of Fact to Matters of Concern' *Critical Inquiry* 30(2): 225–248

Latour, Bruno 2014 'Agency at the Time of the Anthropocene' *New Literary History* 45(1): 1–18

Latour, Bruno 2017 'Why Gaia Is Not a God of Totality' *Theory, Culture, and Society* 34: 61–81

Latour, Bruno 2018 *Facing Gaia: Eight Lectures on the New Climatic Regime*, Catherine Porter trans, Polity

Latour, Bruno and Timothy Lenton 2019 'Extending the Domain of Freedom, or Why Gaia Is So Hard to Understand' *Critical Inquiry* 45: 659–680

Lauer, Christopher 2012 *The Suspension of Reason in Hegel and Schelling*, Bloomsbury Publishing

Law, John 2015 'What's Wrong with a One-World World?' *Distinktion: Scandinavian Journal of Social Theory* 16(1): 126–139

Law, John and Marianne Lien 2018 'Denaturalizing Nature' in Marisol de la Cadena and Mario Blaser eds *A World of Many Worlds*, Duke University Press

Lennox, James 1994 'Teleology by Another Name: A Reply to Ghiselin' *Biology and Philosophy* 9(4): 493–495

Leunissen, Mariska 2010 *Explanation and Teleology in Aristotle's Science of Nature*, Cambridge University Press

Limon, Cressida 2013 'Inventing Animals' in Yoriko Otomo and Edward Mussawir eds *Law and the Question of the Animal*, Glasshouse

Linton, Jamie and Jessica Budds 2014 'The Hydrosocial Cycle: Defining and Mobilizing a Relational-Dialectical Approach to Water' *Geoforum* 57: 170–180

Llewellyn, Karl 1931 'Some Realism About Realism – Responding to Dean Pound' *Harvard Law Review* 44: 1222–1264

Lloyd, Genevieve 1984 *The Man of Reason: 'Male' and 'Female' in Western Philosophy*, Methuen

Lloyd, Sarah 2018 *Where the Slime Mould Creeps*, Tympanocryptis Press

Lovelock, James E and Lynn Margulis 1974 'Atmospheric Homeostasis by and for the Biosphere: The Gaia Hypothesis' *Tellus* 26(1–2): 2–10

Lucretius 2001 *On the Nature of Things (De Rerum Natura)*, Martin Ferguson Smith trans, Hackett Publishing

Lugones, María 1987 'Playfulness, "World"-Travelling, and Loving Perception' *Hypatia* 2: 3–19

Luhmann, Niklas 1992 'Operational Closure and Structural Coupling: The Differentiation of the Legal System' *Cardozo Law Review* 13: 1419–1441

Lyotard, Jean-François and Jean-Loup Thébaud 1985 *Just Gaming*, Wlad Godzich trans, University of Minnesota Press

Machery, Edouard 2012 'Why I Stopped Worrying About a Definition of Life . . . and Why You Should as Well' *Synthese* 185: 145–164

Macneil, Ian 1999 'Relational Contract Theory: Challenges and Queries' *Northwestern University Law Review* 94(3): 877–907

MacNeil, William 2018 'Boundary, Crossing, Pathway: Margaret Davies' Province of Jurisprudence Undetermined' *Australian Journal of Legal Philosophy* 43: 135–139

Malabou, Catherine 2008 *What Should We Do with Our Brain?*, Sebastian Rand trans, Fordham University Press

Malafouris, Lambros 2010 'Metaplasticity and the Human Becoming: Principles of Neuroarchaeology' *Journal of Anthropological Sciences* 88: 49–72

Malafouris, Lambros 2013 *How Things Shape the Mind*, MIT Press

Marchetti, Giancarlo and Sarin Marchetti eds 2017 *Facts and Values: The Ethics and Metaphysics of Normativity*, Routledge

Margulis, Lynn 1967 'On the Origin of Mitosing Cells' *Journal of Theoretical Biology* 14(3): 225–274

Margulis, Lynn 2001 'The Conscious Cell' *Annals of the New York Academy of Science* 929(1): 55–70

Margulis, Lynn 2010 'Symbiogenesis: A New Principle of Evolution Rediscovery of Boris Mikhaylovich Kozo-Polyansky (1890–1957)' *Paleontological Journal* 44(12): 1525–1539

Margulis, Lynn and James E Lovelock 1974 'Biological Modulation of the Earth's Atmosphere' *Icarus* 21: 471–489

Margulis, Lynn and Dorion Sagan 1995 *What Is Life?*, Weidenfeld and Nicolson

Martuwarra RiverOfLife, Anne Poelina, Donna Bagnall, and Michelle Lim 2020 'Recognizing the Martuwarra's First Law Right to Life as a Living Ancestral Being' *Transnational Environmental Law* 9(3): 541–568

Marwani, Renisa 2019 'Insect Wars: Bees, Bedbugs, and Biopolitics' in Andreas Philippopoulos-Mihalopoulos ed *Routledge Handbook of Law and Theory*, Routledge

Maturana, Humberto R and Francisco Varela 1980 *Autopoiesis and Cognition: The Realization of the Living*, D Reidel

Mayr, Ernst 1974 'Teleological and Teleonomic: A New Analysis' *Boston Studies in the Philosophy of Science* 14: 91–117

McGee, Kyle 2015 'The Fragile Force of Law: Mediation, Stratification, and Law's Material Life' *Law, Culture and the Humanities* 11(3): 467–490

Melissaris, Emmanuel 2009 *Ubiquitous Law: Legal Theory and the Space for Legal Pluralism*, Ashgate

Merchant, Carolyn 1980 *The Death of Nature: Women, Ecology, and the Scientific Revolution*, Harper Collins

Mol, Anemarie 1998 'Lived Realities and the Multiplicity of Norms: A Critical Tribute to George Canguilhem' *Economy and Society* 27(2–3): 274–284

Moskovitch, Katia 2018 'Slime Molds Remember – But Do They Learn?' *Quanta Magazine*, July 9, www.quantamagazine.org/slime-molds-remember-but-do-they-learn-20180709/

Murray, Jamie 2008 'Complexity Theory and Socio-Legal Studies' *Liverpool Law Review* 29: 227–246

Murray, Jamie, Thomas Webb and Stephen Wheatley eds 2019 *Complexity Theory and Law: Mapping an Emergent Jurisprudence*, Routledge

Nedelsky, Jennifer 2012 *Law's Relations: A Relational Theory of Self, Autonomy, and Law*, Oxford University Press

Neimanis, Astrida 2009 'Bodies of Water, Human Rights, and the Hydrocommons' *Topia: Canadian Journal of Cultural Studies* 21: 161–182

Nicholson, Daniel 2018 'Reconceptualising the Organism: From Complex Machine to Flowing Stream' in Daniel J Nicholson and John Dupré eds *Everything Flows: Towards a Processual Philosophy of Biology*, Oxford University Press

Nicholson, Daniel J and John Dupré eds 2018 *Everything Flows: Towards a Processual Philosophy of Biology*, Oxford University Press

Norman, Jana 2021 *Posthuman Legal Subjectivity: Reimagining the Human in the Anthropocene*, Routledge

Nunn, Kenneth 1997 'Law as a Eurocentric Enterprise' *Law and Inequality* 15: 323–371

O'Donnell, Erin 2019 *Legal Rights for Rivers: Competition, Obligation, and Water Governance*, Routledge

O'Donnell, Erin, Anne Poelina, Alessandro Pelizzon, and Cristy Clark 2020 'Stop Burying the Lede: The Essential Role of Indigenous Law(s) in Creating Rights of Nature' *Transnational Environmental Law* 9: 403–427

O'Donnell, Tayanah, Daniel Robinson and Josephine Gillespie eds 2020 *Legal Geography: Perspectives and Methods*, Routledge

O'Donovan, Katherine 1985 *Sexual Divisions in Law*, Weidenfeld and Nicholson

Okrent, Mark 2017 *Nature and Normativity: Biology, Teleology, and Meaning*, Routledge

Otomo, Yoriko and Edward Mussawir eds 2013 *Law and the Question of the Animal*, Glasshouse

Parker, Christine and Fiona Haines 2018 'An Ecological Approach to Regulatory Studies?' *Journal of Law and Society* 45(1): 136–155

Pelizzon, Alessandro 2020 'An Intergenerational Ecological Jurisprudence: The Supreme Court of Colombia and the Rights of the Amazon Rainforest' *Law, Technology and Humans* 2: 33–44

Pelizzon, Alessandro and Aidan Ricketts 2015 'Beyond Anthropocentrism and Back Again: From Ontological to Normative Anthropocentrism' *Australasian Journal of Natural Resources Law and Policy* 18(2): 105–124

Petersmann, Marie-Catherine 2021 'Sympoietic Thinking and Earth-System Law: The Earth, Its Subjects, and the Law' *Earth System Governance* 9: 100114, https://doi.org/10.1016/j.esg.2021.100114

Peterson, Keith 2004 'Translator's Introduction' in Friedrich Wilhelm Joseph von Schelling *First Outline of a System of the Philosophy of Nature*, first published 1799, Keith Peterson trans, SUNY Press

Philippopoulos-Mihalopoulos, Andreas 2013 'The Normativity of an Animal Atmosphere' in Yoriko Otomo and Edward Mussawir eds *Law and the Question of the Animal: A Critical Jurisprudence*, Routledge

Philippopoulos-Mihalopoulos, Andreas 2014 'Critical Autopoiesis and the Materiality of Law' *International Journal of the Semiotics of Law* 27: 389–418

Philippopoulos-Mihalopoulos, Andreas 2015 *Spatial Justice: Body, Lawscape, Atmosphere*, Routledge

Plessner, Helmuth 2019 *Levels of Organic Life and the Human: An Introduction to Philosophical Anthropology*, first published 1928, Millay Hyatt trans, Fordham University Press

Plumwood, Val 1993 *Feminism and the Mastery of Nature*, Routledge

Pocock, JGA 1957 *The Ancient Constitution and the Feudal Law*, Norton

Postema, Gerald 1989 *Bentham and the Common Law Tradition*, Clarendon Press

Pottage, Alain 1998 'The Inscription of Life in Law: Genes, Patents and Biopolitics' *Modern Law Review* 61: 740–765

Pottage, Alain 2015 'Autoplasticity' in Brenna Bhandar and Jon Goldberg-Hillier eds *Plastic Materialities: Politics, Metamorphosis, and Legality in the Work of Catherine Malabou*, Duke University Press

Pound, Roscoe 1910 'Law in Books and Law in Action' *American Law Review* 12: 12–26

Povinelli, Elizabeth 2016 *Geontologies: A Requiem to Late Liberalism*, Duke University Press

Prigogine, Ilya 1997 *The End of Certainty: Time, Chaos, and the New Laws of Nature*, Free Press

Prigogine, Ilya and Isabelle Stengers 1984 *Order out of Chaos: Man's New Dialogue with Nature*, Bantam Books

Pross, Addy 2008 'How Can a Chemical System Act Purposefully? Bridging Between Life and Non-Life' *Journal of Physical Organic Chemistry* 21: 724–730

Putnam, Ruth Anna 2017 'Reflections Concerning Moral Objectivity' in Giancarlo Marchetti and Sarin Marchetti eds *Facts and Values: The Ethics and Metaphysics of Normativity*, Routledge

Rand, Sebastian 2011 'Organism, Normativity, Plasticity: Canguilhem, Kant, Malabou' *Continental Philosophy Review* 44: 341–357

Reid et al 2012 'Slime Mold Uses an Externalized Spatial "Memory" to Navigate in Complex Environments' *Proceedings of the National Academy of Sciences (US)* 109(43): 17490–17494

Resnick, Brian 2018 'Trump Doesn't Have a Science Adviser: This Slime Mold Is Available' *Vox*, April 5, www.vox.com/science-and-health/2018/3/6/17072380/slime-mold-intelligence-hampshire-college

Robinson, Daniel and Margaret Raven 2020 'Recognising Indigenous Customary Law of Totemic Plant Species: Challenges and Pathways' *Geographical Journal* 186: 31–44

Roncancio, Ivan Dario Vargas 2017 'Plants and the Law: Vegetal Ontologies and the Rights of Nature. A Perspective from South America' *Australian Feminist Law Journal* 43(1): 67–87

Rovelli, Carlo 2018 *The Order of Time*, Erica Segre and Simon Carnell trans, Penguin

Ruhl, JB 1996 'The Fitness of Law: Using Complexity Theory to Describe the Evolution of Law and Society and Its Practical Meaning for Democracy' *Vanderbilt Law Review* 49: 1407–1490

Ryan, Lyndall et al 2019 'Colonial Frontiers Massacre Map' in *Colonial Frontier Massacres in Australia, 1788–1930*, University of Newcastle, https://c21ch.newcastle.edu.au/colonialmassacres/map.php

Sagan, Dorion and Lynn Margulis 2013 '"Wind at Life's Back" – Toward a Naturalistic, Whiteheadian Teleology: Symbiogenesis and the Second Law' in Brian G Henning and Adam Scarfe eds *Beyond Mechanism: Putting Life Back into Biology*, Lexington Books

Sandford, Stella 2018 'Kant, Race, and Natural History' *Philosophy and Social Criticism* 44: 950–977

Sarat, Austin 1990 '". . . The Law is All Over": Power, Resistance, and the Legal Consciousness of the Welfare Poor' *Yale Journal of Law & the Humanities* 2(2): 343–379

Schelling, Friedrich Wilhelm Joseph von 1989 *Ideas for a Philosophy of Nature*, first published 1797, Errol Harris and Peter Heath trans, Cambridge University Press

Schelling, Friedrich Wilhelm Joseph von 2004 *First Outline of a System of the Philosophy of Nature*, first published 1799, Keith Peterson trans, SUNY Press

Schneider, ED and JJ Kay 1994 'Life as a Manifestation of the Second Law of Thermodynamics' *Mathematical and Computer Modelling* 19(6–8): 25–28

Schneider, Eric D and Dorion Sagan 2005 *Into the Cool: Energy Flow, Thermodynamics, and Life*, University of Chicago Press

Schrödinger, Erwin 1992 *What Is Life?*, first published 1944, Cambridge University Press

Serres, Michel 1992 *The Natural Contract*, Elizabeth MacArthur and William Paulson trans, University of Michigan Press

Serres, Michel 2000 *The Birth of Physics*, first published 1977, Jack Hawkes trans, David Webb ed, Clinamen Press

Simard, Suzanne 2018 'Mycorrhizal Networks Facilitate Tree Communication, Learning, and Memory' in Frantisek Baluska, Monica Gagliano, and Guenther Witzany eds *Memory and Learning in Plants*, Springer

Simard, Susanne et al 2012 'Mycorrhizal Networks: Mechanisms, Ecology, and Modelling' *Fungal Biology Reviews* 26: 39–60

Stengers, Isabelle 2010 *Cosmopolitics I*, Robert Bononno trans, University of Minnesota Press

Stengers, Isabelle 2011 *Cosmopolitics II*, Robert Bononno trans, University of Minnesota Press

Stolzenberg, Nomi 2010 'Facts on the Ground' in Eduardo Peñalver and Gregory Alexander eds *Property and Community*, Oxford University Press

Sutrop, Urmas 2001 'Umwelt – Word and Concept: Two Hundred Years of Semantic Change' *Semiotica* 134(1): 447–462

Swyngedouw, Erik 1999 'Modernity and Hybridity: Nature, Regeneracionismo, and the Production of the Spanish Waterscape 1890–1930' *Annals of the Association of American Geographers* 89: 443–465

Talcott, Samuel 2019 *Georges Canguilhem and the Problem of Error*, Palgrave Macmillan

Tănăsescu, Mihnea 2020 'Rights of Nature, Legal Personality, and Indigenous Philosophies' *Transnational Environmental Law* 9(3): 429–453

Teubner, Gunther 1992 'The Two Faces of Janus: Rethinking Legal Pluralism' *Cardozo Law Review* 13: 1443–1462

Todes, Daniel 1987 'Darwin's Malthusian Metaphor and Russian Evolutionary Thought, 1859–1917' *Isis* 78(4): 537–551

Tomas, Nin 2011 'Maori Concepts of Rangatiratanga, Kaitiakitanga, the Environment and Property Rights' in David Grinlinton and Prue Taylor eds *Property Rights and Sustainability: The Evolution of Property Rights to Meet Ecological Challenges*, Martinus Nijhoff

Turner, Bethaney and Wendy Somerville 2020 'Composting with Cullunghutti: Experimenting with How to Meet a Mountain' *Journal of Australian Studies* 44(2): 224–242

Turner, J Scott 2013 'Biology's Second Law: Homeostasis, Purpose, and Desire' in Brian Henning and Adam Scarfe eds *Beyond Mechanism: Putting Life Back into Biology*, Lexington Books

Uexküll, Jakob von 1926 *Theoretical Biology*, DL MacKinnon trans, Harcourt, Brace, and Co

Uexküll, Jakob von 1982 'The Theory of Meaning' *Semiotica* 42(1): 25–82

Uexküll, Jakob von 2010 *A Foray into the Worlds of Animals and Humans, with a Theory of Meaning*, first published 1934, Joseph D O'Neill trans, University of Minnesota Press

Valverde, Mariana 2006 'The Sociology of Law as a "Means Against Struggle Itself"' *Social and Legal Studies* 15: 591–597

Valverde, Mariana 2015 *Chronotopes of Law: Jurisdiction, Scale and Governance*, Routledge

Van den Berg, Hein 2014 *Kant on Proper Science: Biology in the Critical Philosophy and the Opus Postumum*, Springer

Van Klink, Bart 2009 'Facts and Norms: The Unfinished Debate Between Eugen Ehrlich and Hans Kelsen' in Marc Hertogh ed *Living Law: Reconsidering Eugen Ehrlich*, Hart Publishing

Veitch, Scott 2021 *Obligations*, Routledge

Verran, Helen 2018 'The Politics of Working Cosmologies Together While Keeping Them Separate' in Marisol de la Cadena and Mario Blaser eds *A World of Many Worlds*, Duke University Press

Von Benda-Beckmann, Keebet and Bertram Turner 2018 'Legal Pluralism, Social Theory, and the State' *Journal of Legal Pluralism and Unofficial Law* 50(3): 255–274

Watson, Irene 2000 'Kaldowinyeri – Munaintya, In the Beginning' *Flinders Journal of Law Reform* 4: 3–17

Watson, Irene 2017 'Aboriginal Laws of the Land: Surviving Fracking, Golf Courses and Drains Among Other Extractive Industries' in Nicole Rogers and Michelle Maloney eds *Law as If Earth Really Mattered: The Wild Law Judgment Project*, Routledge

Webb, David 2000 'Introduction' in Jack Hawkes trans, David Webb and Michel Serres eds *The Birth of Physics*, Clinamen Press

Whitehead, Alfred North 1938 *Modes of Thought*, Free Press

Wilcox, Christie 2019 'How Jurassic Plankton Stole Control of the Ocean's Chemistry' *Quanta Magazine*, October 1, www.quantamagazine.org/how-jurassic-plankton-stole-control-of-the-oceans-chemistry-20191001/

Woese, Carl 2004 'A New Biology for a New Century' *Microbiology and Molecular Biology Reviews* 68(2): 173–186

Wolfe, Charles 2014 'Holism, Organicism and the Risk of Biochauvinism' *Verifiche* 43(1–3): 41–76

Wolfe, Charles 2015 'Was Canguilhem a Biochauvinist? Goldstein, Canguilhem and the Project of Biophilosophy' in D Meacham ed *Medicine and Society, New Perspectives in Continental Philosophy*, Springer

Wright, Kate 2020 'Rhythms of Law: Aboriginal Jurisprudence and the Anthropocene' *Law and Critique* 31: 293–308

Yusoff, Kathryn 2013 'Insensible Worlds: Postrelational Ethics, Indeterminacy and the (K)nots of Relating' *Environment and Planning D* 31: 208–226

Zartaloudis, Thanos 2019 *The Birth of Nomos*, Edinburgh University Press

Index

126 *Index*

For Product Safety Concerns and Information please contact our EU
representative GPSR@taylorandfrancis.com
Taylor & Francis Verlag GmbH, Kaufingerstraße 24, 80331 München, Germany